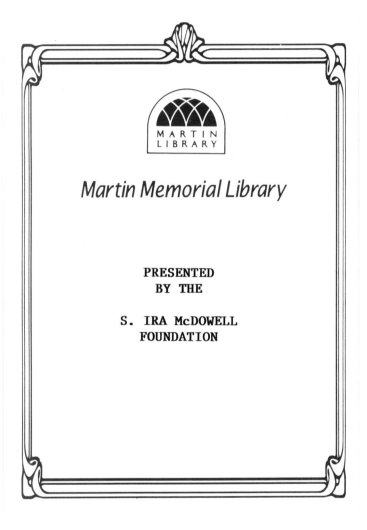

MARTIN
LIBRARY

Martin Memorial Library

Also by Jack Nicklaus

My 55 Ways to Lower Your Golf Score

Take a Tip from Me

The Greatest Game of All (with Herbert Warren Wind)

Golf My Way (with Ken Bowden)

Jack Nicklaus' Lesson Tee (with Ken Bowden)

On and Off the Fairway (with Ken Bowden)

Jack Nicklaus' Playing Lessons (with Ken Bowden)

The Full Swing (with Ken Bowden)

My Most Memorable Shots in the Majors (with Ken Bowden)

My Story (with Ken Bowden)

Paperback
(with Ken Bowden and Jim McQueen)

Play Better Golf: The Swing from A–Z

Play Better Golf: The Short Game and Scoring

Play Better Golf: Short Cuts to Lower Scores

JACK NICKLAUS
My Golden
Lessons

100-PLUS WAYS TO IMPROVE YOUR SHOTS, LOWER YOUR SCORES, AND ENJOY GOLF MUCH, MUCH MORE

JACK NICKLAUS WITH KEN BOWDEN
Illustrations by Jim McQueen

Simon & Schuster
NEW YORK   LONDON   TORONTO   SYDNEY   SINGAPORE

SIMON & SCHUSTER
Rockefeller Center
1230 Avenue of the Americas
New York, NY 11020

SIMON & SCHUSTER and colophon are registered trademarks
of Simon & Schuster, Inc.

For information regarding special discounts for bulk purchasers, please contact
Simon & Schuster Special Sales at 1-800-456-6798 or business@simonandschuster.com

Designed by Hasak Publishing, Inc.

Manufactured in the United States of America

1   3   5   7   9   10   8   6   4   2

Library of Congress Cataloging-in-Publication Data is available.

ISBN 0-7432-4107-X

To JIM McQUEEN

Good friend, excellent golfer, and outstanding artist,
who has captured my likeness better than anyone.

Contents

The Best of My Own Best Lessons

MOST GOLF INSTRUCTION BOOKS attempt to be what might be called "A to Z," taking students through every facet of playing the game in, hopefully, a logically sequential order. They are, of course, ideal for beginners and relatively inexperienced players.

This is not that kind of book.

This is a book for refining the game you already have; for solving your problems, major or minor; for strengthening your weaknesses and clearing up your confusions. Most of all, its goal is to help you become more expert and adept in how you swing your clubs and think about and play a great many of your shots.

It developed into that kind of book because of the way it was created.

From the spring of 1988 through early 2001, I contributed a "how-to" tip a month initially to *Golf Digest* and then to *Golf Magazine*.

My objective was the same throughout both series.

It was to pass on to improvement-conscious golfers those elements of physical technique and mental approach that I believe helped me the most during my competitive career, all the way from my amateur days to those of professional senior golf.

In other words, what I attempted to recall and put on paper was the best of my own best "lessons"—the cream of the crop from a lifetime of studying, learning, and endlessly trying to improve at golf.

Each tip in the series was self-contained, dealing with a single and often a finer point of the game. In working with Ken Bowden on the words, I also did my best to stick to the point—that is, to deliver my advice as clearly and concisely as possible, subject only to making it easily understood by all levels of players.

Accordingly, you will find the texts herein in many instances relatively short—leaving plenty of space for the many wonderful illustrations of "key" actions by the renowned artist Jim McQueen. Once a golf professional himself, Jim, like Ken, has worked with me on many publishing projects in the past.

The subjects of the lessons as we proceeded remained random—pretty much, whatever came to mind at any given time. For ease of reference in book form, however, we have ordered the articles more or less thematically, beginning with those all-important pre-swing fundamentals, concluding the one-pagers with getting the ball in the hole, and finally, offering some guidance for better players.

In putting these materials together, we discovered that, haphazardly as we selected subjects for the magazine series', when we completed assembling this book we had covered just about every element of the game necessary to becoming a better player.

My thanks to *Golf Digest* and *Golf Magazine* for their cooperation in this project, and to my lifelong publisher, Simon & Schuster, for again excelling at what they have done so well for so long.

OCTOBER, 2002

JACK NICKLAUS

My Golden Lessons

EQUIPMENT

LITTLE CAN REPLACE sound instruction and advice from a qualified teaching professional, but you can defeat your goal of improving your golf game if playing the wrong equipment. And, the better player you become, the more important it becomes to ensure that your equipment is a perfect fit.

Experience is a big factor in choosing the right equipment, as can be advice from a golf professional who knows your physical make-up, your playing tendencies, your strengths and weaknesses, and your ultimate goals in the game.

In the end, though, and because of the numerous options available to players these days, finding the right clubs and your ideal ball becomes largely a matter of trial and error. Few people buy a car without first test-driving it, and the same could be said for golf equipment. If you are fortunate enough to be a member of a club, take full advantage of the opportunities to try your golf shop's demo clubs, be it a driver, a wedge or a putter. If you are out playing a weekend round with friends, take your buddy up on that offer to try his or her new driver or that latest putter. You might find something to your liking, and something that will ultimately improve your game.

When it comes to balls, the choices are now so numerous that they have become almost confusing. Because of stringent guidelines and quality control, the reality is there's hardly a bad ball out there these days. So, over time, be sure to try as many types and brands as possible, until you find a ball with which you are most comfortable. Certainly, you can try to marry ball compression to your swing speed, but, in the end, if you like the distance you are getting from the ball, the playability, and the "feel" at impact, you have probably found the right ball for you.

Play the Ideal Ball for You

WITH TODAY'S HUGE VARIETY of interior structures, cover materials, dimple patterns, and distance/durability claims, I'm sure many golfers find it hard to decide which golf ball to play. However, one part of the puzzle remains easy to solve: compression.

I'm told that scientists have proven that, under optimum conditions, the highest compression balls always go the farthest. Even if that's true—and I find it hard to believe—there's much more to playing good golf than raw distance.

To a slow or easy-swinging golfer, or one achieving only a modest percentage of center hits, the highest (100) compression ball will feel like a rock. To a very hard-hitting player who flushes most shots, a softer ball (90 or lower) will feel mushy and unresponsive. Because feel is such an important factor in golf, the psychological impact of both mismatches is likely to be negative.

If your pro knows your game, he'll know the right compression ball for you—although you may have to get your ego out of the way to accept his advice. To help you, consider that although most Tour players use 100 compression balls, quite a few go with 90, or even lower nowadays as compressions have diminished.

As you make feel the decisive factor in compression choice, apply it also to ball composition. There's no question that the greater impact feel and feedback of the softer balls make them easier to play around the greens. Overall, though, the more comfortable you feel about what you're hitting—be it balata, a hard-covered wound ball, a soft-covered two-piece ball, or those ultra-durable supposed "rockets"—the better you'll hit it.

Fit Your Grips to Your Shot Pattern

NO AMOUNT OF MONEY can buy you a first-class golf game, but spending a few dollars to experiment with grip size could improve the one you've got—possibly quite a lot.

If your natural or desired flight pattern is right-to-left, grips on the thin side will make it easier for you to use the clubhead more aggressively through brisker wrist action. Conversely, if your tendency or taste is to move the ball primarily left-to-right, fattening your grips will help you to restrain the clubhead through reduced wrist action.

As a fader of the ball during most of my peak years, I favored slightly oversized grips even though I have small hands. As I've gotten older and faced the challenge of keeping up my clubhead speed and needing to draw more shots for distance, I've gradually reduced my grip thickness.

Any golf professional can give you a different size grip in a matter of minutes. Experiment at first with just one or two favorite clubs, then match the rest of your set to the size that works best.

Find the Right Driver

FINDING THE DRIVER that best suits your physique and swing pattern will help you hit more fairways and shorten your approach shots. With all the technological options available today, just about everyone's ideal club is out there somewhere. Working with a knowledge-able golf professional will shorten the search, especially if he or she has trial clubs on hand. Here are a few guidelines to get you started.

If you have adequate or exceptional length, focus on maximizing your carry. Since high-flying, soft-landing shots allow you to better control where the ball ends up, a longer carry is a major plus for you. And, by promoting a high fade, a relatively firm shaft and a square or even slightly open clubface also could be beneficial.

If you're a short hitter, try to produce a lower ball flight and more roll. A lower-lofted club with a regular or flexible shaft, as well as a slightly closed clubface, will promote a hotter-running draw.

With so many brands to choose from, you'll likely end up having to decide between similar models. Because eye appeal is a definite psychological factor, go with the club that "looks" the best to you; if you're not comfortable with a club's appearance, it will never work.

Make a Friend of Your Sand Wedge

I'M NOT PREPARED to take another club out of my bag to make room for a 60-degree or "lob" wedge. So, instead, I use a weak-lofted, 58-degree, sand wedge. Even though it's called a sand wedge, I've always used it for many more shots than those from bunkers. So should you—particularly if you don't carry a third wedge.

Even if your sand wedge carries only the standard 56 degrees of loft, it's still a better choice than the pitching wedge for those short pitch shots that must fly high and spin to a quick stop. Because you can swing it harder than the pitching wedge—and therefore are less likely to decelerate into impact—

you'll often get better results with the sand wedge from about 65 yards and in.

From the rough, sandy turf, pine needles, and other loose impediments, the heavy-bladed, deep-flanged sand wedge slides under the ball more easily than a pitching wedge.

The sand wedge also is the best club for playing short downhill chips from just off the green.

Believe me, the friendlier you become with your sand wedge, the more shots it will take off your score.

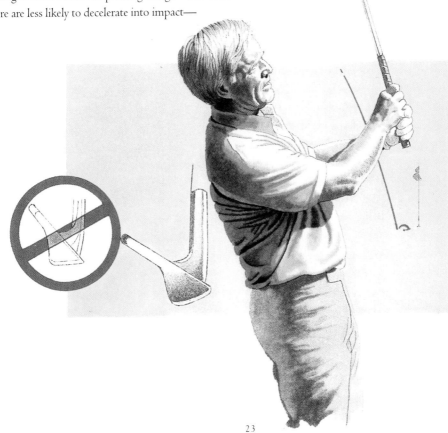

Start Youngsters with the Correct Clubs

THERE ARE THREE WAYS to equip young beginning golfers. You can give them adult clubs, adult clubs cut down in the shaft, or buy them specially built junior clubs.

Junior clubs are almost always the only ones a very young child can handle. However, when considering them, be prepared for the youngster to outgrow them faster than you might think. Also, be sure you seek out quality—there are some flimsy versions around.

As the child grows bigger and stronger, I recommend moving him to full-sized adult clubs as soon as possible. Children will build golf muscles and master good swing basics faster that way. This was certainly true with my kids, all five of whom actually started out with the lightest versions of adult clubs.

If you go to cut-down adult clubs as a transition, forget anything you may have heard about them being too heavy for all but the strongest youngsters. The truth is, the shorter the shaft, the lower the swing-weight of the club, which means the lighter its dynamic—in action and feel.

When considering cost factors, keep in mind that a child who isn't having any fun with golf due to improper or shoddy equipment isn't likely to stick with the game for very long.

Take Good Care of Your Tools

EVER NOTICE HOW METICULOUS Tour caddies are about cleaning their players' clubs? First thing every caddie does when he gets a club back after the playing of a shot is carefully wipe off its face with a wet towel. The reason, of course, beyond a certain esthetic concern, is to ensure the removal of dirt or grass from within the grooves, which could affect the spin of the ball the next time the club is used.

You may not want to go to that much trouble when you're playing the course, but I suggest you always have your clubfaces cleaned or do it yourself after a round or a practice session. You'll definitely feel better looking down at a clean clubface than a

dirty one, and, if you make the right swing, the ball will have a better chance of behaving as you intend.

Look to your grips, also. Gary Player, in the days I traveled with him a lot, would wash his rubber grips with detergent every evening to be sure they'd be fresh and tacky for the next day's play. Watch Fred Couples in a tournament and, for the same reason, you'll see him take a towel and wipe off the grip before just about every shot he plays.

Even though you may not believe mucky club-faces and tired grips hurt your game all that much, I doubt if you'd be very happy with what they suggest to other players about your attitude to the game.

BEFORE YOU SWING

I'VE SAID AND WRITTEN many times over the years that golf is 80 percent set-up. The longer I play this game, the more I'm convinced of that assertion's accuracy.

The factors that go into set-up or address include clubface aim, body alignment, head position, stance, posture, and the placement of the ball between the feet and its distance from the body. Many golfers neglect these "statics," because they find them tedious, but they need your constant attention, particularly the first two—clubface aim and body alignment.

After all, when shooting a rifle, you wouldn't expect to hit the target if you didn't aim the rifle correctly at the outset. So, in golf, how can you expect to hit your target without the proper aim?

Many middle- and high-handicappers could save themselves a lot of strokes by learning how to set-up correctly. Frequently, however, these golfers don't like to bother with what they regard as boring "statics," or they give up too quickly on the proper set-up because it feels unnatural at first.

Nevertheless, the truth is that, the better you want to play, the more attention you must pay to what you do before you ever swing the club.

Prepare Your Body Before You Begin

SO YOU NEVER SEEM TO HAVE the time or the inclination to warm up before a round? Then at least give your body the benefit of a little stretching before you attempt to smash that opening tee shot into the wild blue yonder.

I never go into a tournament round without completing a full warm-up and rarely play a casual game without first hitting a few practice balls. At the very least, I go through the stretches illustrated here somewhere between the practice green and the first tee, both as a precaution against injuring myself and as a final warm-up before playing perhaps the most important shot of the day.

I start by making a few full, easy practice swings. Next, I hold the club behind my back and turn to my left and then to my right, first with my arms extended and then with the club held across the middle of my back. Finally, I recommend holding a couple of irons in a baseball grip and making slow swings back and through.

Remember, you want to prepare your body to make good swings right from the first tee, while minimizing the chance of injury.

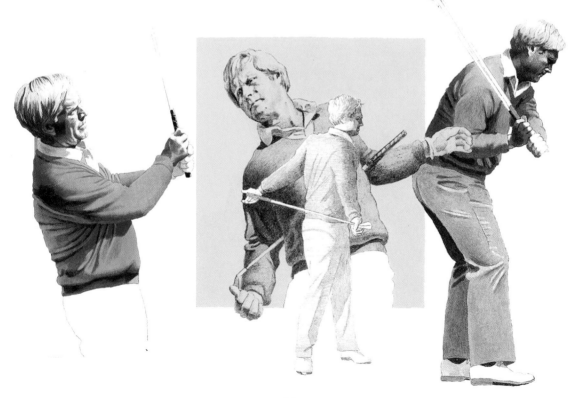

Stay with Fundamentals
Regardless of Height

OLD-TIME GOLF ANALYSTS used to say that Bob Jones, at 5-9, was the ideal height for a golfer. At a couple of inches taller than that, I've felt that my extra height was an asset in helping me create a bigger swing arc.

You'll see some very tall golfers going through all kinds of contortions—slouched shoulders, deep knee bends—to get themselves into what they think are effective address positions. What many don't seem to realize is that, whatever their height, their hands probably hang at pretty much the same distance from the ground as everyone else's, which explains why the majority of golfers are well suited to standard-length clubs.

Thus, with few exceptions, there's little relationship between height and shaft length. Tall golfers may need their clubs to lie more upright to promote correct posture, but beyond that they should forget about compensations either in their equipment or technique. Properly mastered, the fundamentals of the game will work as well for them as for anyone else, both at address and during the swing.

The same applies to short golfers, with the possible exception that slightly longer shafts may help them achieve a bigger swing arc, and that they may need their clubs to lie a little flatter.

Make Your Grip
Harmonize Your Hands

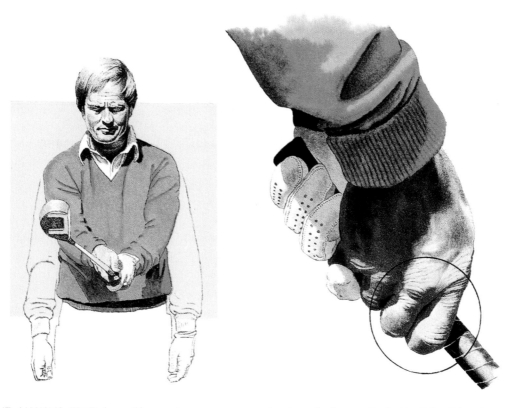

I'VE ALWAYS FELT that golfers tend to get too nit-picky about how many knuckles are visible, or where the "Vs" of the thumbs and forefingers point when the grip is completed. If you stand erect with your arms hanging freely at your sides, then extend them forward and wrap your hands easily around the club, without any twisting or manipulating, you'll never go far wrong in terms of hand alignment.

The most important thing about the grip is that the hands don't fight each other during the swing—they should work together in total harmony. This makes how the fingers take hold of the club at least as important as hand alignment.

The more space your fingers occupy on the club, the harder it will be for your hands to function as a single unit. Put another way, the fingers of both hands, as well as the hands themselves, should be as close together as you can comfortably get them.

In this regard, be particularly careful about your right forefinger. You might be tempted to set it well apart from its brethren in a "triggered" position, but I think you'll better "unitize" your grip by keeping it snug against your middle finger.

Find the Link that Works Best for You

AN EFFECTIVE, COMFORTABLE GRIP is critical in golf, so don't be afraid to experiment with different options to find the best grip for you. The quality of your shots will tell you what works and what doesn't.

As a youngster, I tried the overlapping, or Vardon, grip used by most golfers, in which the right-hand pinkie finger curls over or around the left forefinger. In developing my game, however, I soon found that my dad's way of holding the club—interlocking the right pinkie with the left forefinger—worked better for me. The fact that I have small hands was probably a factor in my choice of the interlocking grip.

A third option is the 10-finger, or baseball, grip, in which all the fingers of both hands hold the club. Bob Rosburg and Beth Daniel are among the players who have excelled using this type of grip.

As you seek your own ideal grip, remember that any change will feel uncomfortable at first and will need a fair trial. Try different grips on the practice range first until you feel comfortable enough to take your new grip to the course.

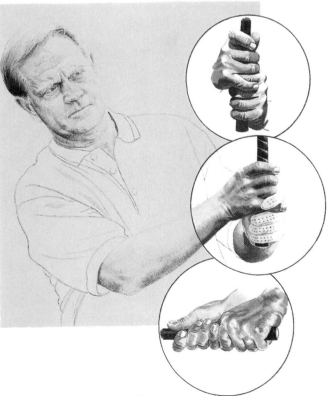

Always Follow This Set-up Procedure

HERE'S A SIMPLE TIP on the set-up that will put you in position to hit your targets. Address the ball correctly by following this procedure: 1) square the clubface; 2) set your hands correctly on the grip; 3) position your body. Many golfers take their grip and stance first and then lower the clubhead to the ball. This, however, makes precise clubface aim difficult.

Instead, have a well-ordered plan. With the club in your leading hand only, set the bottom edge of the clubface perpendicular to your target line. This points the clubface directly at your target. Once you've correctly aimed the clubface, carefully add

your trailing hand to the grip, making sure not to disrupt the clubface aim. Finally, square your body to the target line you've just used to aim the clubface.

Keep in mind that squaring the clubface directly to the target applies only when you're attempting to hit a dead-straight shot. When you want to fade the ball from left to right, point the clubface slightly right of the target, or open. Conversely, when intending a draw, point the clubface slightly left of the target, or closed.

Even if you change your clubface aim from shot to shot, keep the procedure the same. Follow the right order and you'll hit better, more consistent shots.

Keep a Steady Head ...

SOME TEACHERS THESE DAYS tell you to let your head move during the swing, while others stick to the old theory of keeping it steady.

What's my take on this?

Leaving my head where I position it at address has been my number-one fundamental ever since Jack Grout taught me to focus on a steady head all those years ago in Columbus, Ohio. Here's why.

For most players, moving the head more than fractionally during the swing costs them both distance and accuracy because it changes the swing plane. If you can exactly and consistently compensate when coming down for whatever you do going back—swaying, dipping, or rising—fine. If not, the penalty is a miss-hit.

But there's a difference between keeping the head steady and absolutely still, which restricts the swinging motion.

Like many good players over the years, I give myself the freedom to make a full arm swing and full upper body turn by rotating my chin an inch or two away from the target as a backswing trigger.

If you give this technique a try, just be sure your head rotates around the top of your spine rather than aimlessly around in space.

...But Position Your Head Naturally

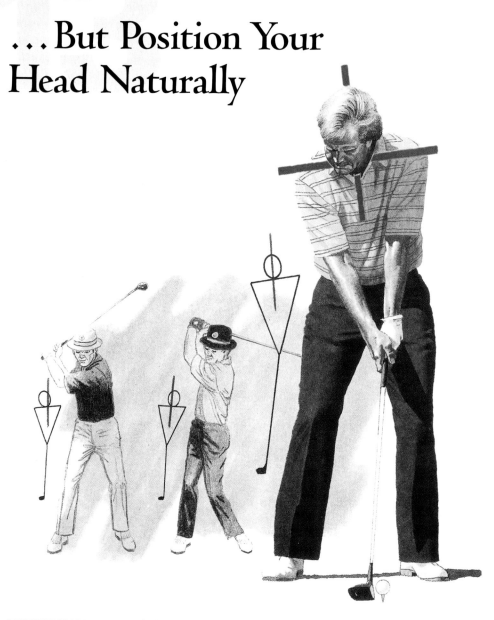

SETTING THE HEAD too far back, away from the target, puts too much weight on the right side. This makes turning the body in the backswing difficult, particularly at the hips. The result is often a short swing or an arms-only swing, and in both cases usually a weak one.

Positioning the head too far forward, or toward the target, sets too much weight on the left side. This makes for overswinging and a reverse pivot—the classic "fire and fall back" action.

The image that most often helps me get this "geometry" right as I set up to the ball is of my head remaining in its most natural position—perpendicular to my shoulders and in the middle of my body.

Tilt the Triangle for Correct Shoulder Slant

MANY OF THE HIGH HANDICAPPERS I happen across seem to have a terrible time setting up with the correct slant to their shoulders at address.

The most frequent problem is setting the shoulders too level, which either forces the right shoulder forward or positions the hands too far back in relation to the ball. Just as destructive is overtilting the shoulders by either forcing the left one up or the right one down.

Here's a mind-picture that will cure both faults:

As you set up, visualize a line connecting your shoulders and join it to imaginary lines running straight down each arm, so that the three lines form the equilateral triangle you see in the illustration.

To assure the correct shoulder inclination on every shot, simply tilt the entire triangle slightly away from the target as you set up to the ball.

Check and Recheck
Your Alignment

THE FIRST THING you should check when your game inexplicably leaves you is your set-up to the ball, particularly your alignment to the target. Since golfers can't readily see their alignment at address, they sometimes slip into poor positions. It's a simple problem that afflicts all golfers, even Tour pros.

Some years ago, I went to the first Senior PGA Tour major of the year, The Tradition, playing poorly. There I consulted Jim Flick, who's frequently worked on my game with me in recent years. After silently watching me hit practice balls for a few minutes, Jim asked me to take my set-up and then stop. He then walked over, slid his feet in where mine were, and had me take a look from behind the ball. He asked where I thought a golfer so aligned would hit it. I told him 30 yards to the right.

But you don't need an instructor to check your alignment. Lay a club just outside and parallel to your target line, then take your address and place another club along your stance line. Step behind the ball: If the shafts are parallel, your alignment is square.

Within five minutes of readjusting my set-up, my shots were flying exactly where I wanted them to. That weekend I shot 65-65 to win The Tradition for the fourth time.

Moral: Never mess with your swing until you're certain you are aimed correctly.

Let Buttons Guide Your Shoulder Alignment

I USE THE BUTTONS on my golf shirt to help me sharpen my mental imagery and physical sensing of the proper shoulder alignment for the shot I want to hit.

When I want to hit straight (**A**), I visualize the buttons being square to the ball both at address and at impact. When I want to fade (**B**), I "see" the buttons as being a little past the ball at both those points. When I want to draw a shot (**C**), the buttons in my mind's eye are set just behind the ball at address and return only to that point through impact.

In my clinics I've found that the last of those images is helpful to golfers who work their shoulders "out and over," rather than "down and under," on the forward swing.

Line 'Em Up to Keep Your Hands Leading

AT IMPACT, players tend to replicate the same positions they held at address. That's an accepted truth in golf. Also widely believed is the notion that the golf ball is struck most accurately and powerfully when the hands are slightly ahead of it.

That being the case, it would seem logical to set up at address with the hands positioned slightly ahead of the ball, or directly opposite it when you're trying to sweep the ball off a tee with the driver.

The easiest way I have found to consistently achieve this hands-leading relationship is to make a straight line from the clubhead to my left shoulder as I set up to the ball.

A bonus of this arrangement is that it promotes a smooth, one-piece takeaway in which no part of the body moves ahead of any other part.

Relax Shoulders to Ease Elbows

ONE OF GOLF'S MYSTERIES among higher handicappers is how the elbows should be arranged at address. You'll see players with their elbows forced so close together they appear to have been tied there. Others twist their arms until the muscles look like coiled rope in an effort to point the elbows at their midriffs.

Ben Hogan and Gary Player both played superbly with what I'd call forced-elbow positions, but I believe most recreational golfers tend to create way too much tension when they become unnatural in any element of the set-up.

For my arms to swing freely back and through, they must feel relaxed and supple at address. I achieve this by consciously drooping or slumping my shoulders as I lean over to the ball, while allowing no more tension in my arms as I position the clubhead than when they hang loosely at my sides.

Achieving these "feels" assures me my elbows are correctly—that is, naturally—positioned. I think it might do the same for you.

Set Up "At Ease" for Free Arm Swing

YOU NEED TO MINIMIZE TENSION in all parts of your body at address, but particularly in your arms. That's impossible unless your shoulders are fully relaxed.

Here's a very simple image, along with a drill, that will produce the desired effect.

When a soldier standing stiffly at attention is given the at-ease order, the first thing that happens is a slumping of the shoulders.

"See" and feel your shoulders behaving just like the soldier's as you set up to each shot, both in practice and in play.

Let them really relax and you'll feel your arms go limp right along with the slumping, which is just the way they should be to make a full, fluid golf swing.

THE FULL SWING

THE MOST FORTUNATE THING that happened to me in golf was starting out with an exceptionally talented teacher, my lifelong friend Jack Grout.

Working with Jack from day one—or, in my case, 10 years old—meant that I began with and continued to play and practice golf with the correct swing fundamentals always in mind. Thus, I never had to waste time and energy later in my career on fixing ingrained mistakes or bad habits. Of course, my technique evolved with age and experience, and I was always willing to listen to advice from players whose talent or knowledge of the game I respected. But, basically, the fundamentals I learned as a youngster from Jack Grout served me beautifully throughout my entire career.

Whether you get advice directly from a teacher, from books or magazines or videos, or any other credible source, be certain to learn and master the swing's long-proven, basic fundamentals—then, stick to them through the thick and thin you'll inevitably encounter in this game.

Take a Lesson Before Restarting the Game

GOLF IS MORE ENJOYABLE when you play well. If you'd like to prove that to yourself once again, do what I did at the start of every new season for most of my career: Take a lesson.

Whether it was January 1st or later, whenever I hauled my clubs from the closet after my fall/winter layoff, I'd call my boyhood teacher and great friend, Jack Grout, and ask him to join me on the practice tee.

Once there, my words never varied: "Okay, Jack, time to teach me golf one more time, starting with the grip, the set-up, the backswing ..." And that's what we would do, from A to Z, almost as though I was a complete beginner.

There were two benefits to this annual drill. First and foremost, those start-over sessions cleared my head of whatever erroneous ideas had lingered from the previous season. Secondly, by getting a complete refresher in the relatively few but critical fundamentals of the game, I felt assured that all the work I would do going forward would be correctly focused.

Today, I have no doubt that my record would have been considerably diminished without that annual discipline. If you would like to enjoy the greatest game of all even more, give it a try.

Always Play to Your Strengths

TRADITIONAL WISDOM SAYS that large, strong hands are essential to playing good golf. If that were true, I'd still be selling insurance for a living. My hands are small and my fingers are short; I wear a small- or medium-cadet golf glove. I even kidded in a book that my wife Barbara has stronger hands than I have from all the housework she does!

There's no question that large, powerful hands have served many players well. Notable examples include Harry Vardon, Tommy Armour, Byron Nelson, and Arnold Palmer. But, I hope my career proves a person can excel at golf without strong hands.

The key, as in other areas where physique is a factor, is to use your natural strengths in the way you swing the golf club to overcome or offset your weaknesses.

For instance, my top physical asset as a youngster was arm and leg strength. In building my game, my teacher, Jack Grout, focused primarily on arm extension and body coil going back, then leading with the lower body coming down, with relatively passive hands throughout.

Employ the same "use-your-strengths" philosophy with your game, ideally with a teacher who knows how to exploit your particular assets.

Forget Trying to Hit Dead Straight Shots

AT THE HIGHEST LEVELS of golf, absolutely straight shots are mere accidents. Does this sound puzzling to you? It's the truth. The best players attempt to either draw or fade the ball slightly on all full shots. Let me explain why.

Since I've preferred to fade the ball for most of my career, let's suppose I set up on the approach shot illustrated here (below right) for 10 feet of left-to-right curvature. If I hit the shot as intended and my distance is exact, the ball finishes at the hole. If, instead, I hit the ball dead straight, I have a 10-foot putt from the left side of the hole. If I fade a little too much, I still leave myself a putt of around 10 feet from the right side of the hole.

Now to my opponent, the supposed straight shooter (far right). If he goes directly for the pin and executes perfectly, he'll be right at the hole. But, if his shot curves to the right or left the same amount as my shot in the last scenario, he leaves himself a 20-footer, twice as bad as

my miss. Should he repeat that error over a full round, he will put himself at a major disadvantage.

The principle involved here applies to hitting fairways, too. It should be clear that playing with either a fade or a draw instead of a straight ball will make you a more consistent golfer. Chances are, you have a natural ball flight—play for it when you plan your shots.

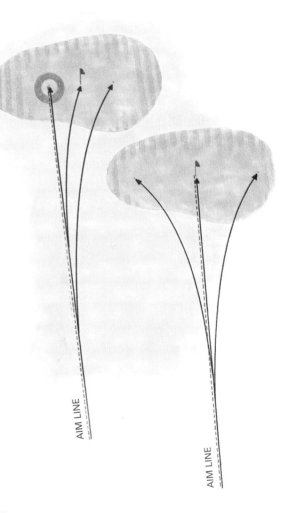

AIM LINE

AIM LINE

Know Your Impact Goal

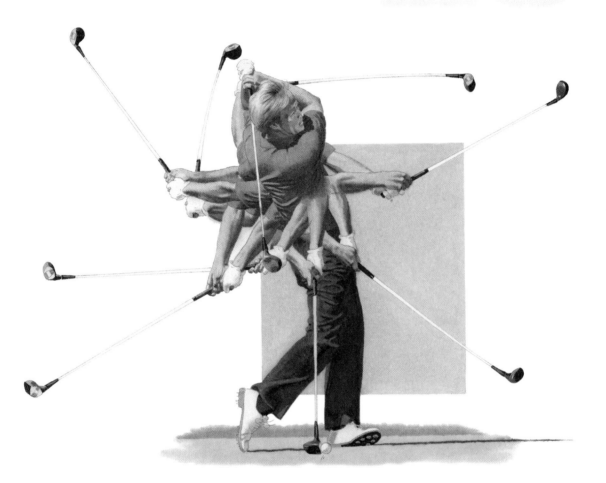

I'M FREQUENTLY ASKED at clinics, invariably by golfers who slice or pull most of their shots, "How do I hit from the inside out?" My answer starts: "Unless you want to draw or hook a shot from right to left, that's not what you should be trying to do."

I then emphasize that knowing and visualizing how the clubhead must be made to behave as it meets the ball to create a particular flight is the first step toward becoming a competent golfer.

For instance, for the ball to fly directly to the target, it must be struck with the clubface square as the clubhead travels from inside the target line, to momentarily straight along that line at impact, to inside again on the follow-through.

Thus, that's the swing goal "picture" you should have in your mind whenever you want to hit directly to your target.

Work with Motion Over Mechanics

IT'S ALL-TOO EASY for golfers looking to improve their swing mechanics to lose sight of the single most important factor in the game: swinging the clubhead. You simply must swing the club freely through the ball.

As long as it promotes this vital motion, training various parts of your body to reach certain positions during the swing can definitely help you play better. When such mechanics in any way inhibit the speed or correct positioning of the clubhead, however, they will always cost you distance or accuracy.

Fluid motion allows you to deliver the clubhead accurately and at a high rate of speed. And this kind of motion can only come from relaxed muscles. So beware of anything mechanical that restricts your muscles. Understand that attaining a particular position during the swing, as ideal as it may seem, is worthless if it interferes with the free use of the clubhead.

Thus, a final tip: Always side with motion over mechanics when you're not sure if a particular swing concept is working for you.

First, "See" All Your Shots

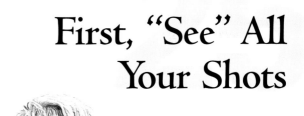

FOR SOME 40 YEARS now, I've gone through the same visualization process before every competitive shot. No other discipline has helped me more, and I'd like to share the process with you here. If your shot execution tends to be careless and inconsistent, visualizing exactly what you want to achieve before setting up and swinging will greatly improve your play.

The more deeply you ingrain what I like to call my "going-to-the-movies" discipline, the more effective you will become at hitting the shots you want to hit. Applying it on the practice tee as well as on the golf course will speed up your mastery of the process. Try this:

First, "see" in your mind's eye where you want the ball to finish. Be realistic about your capabilities, but always imagine positive results, never miss-hits.

Second, "see" the ball flying to the target you've just visualized, to the point of mentally picturing the trajectory, curvature, and roll.

Third, "see" yourself setting up and swinging in such a way as to turn these imaginary pictures into reality.

Fourth, select the club that the completed "movie" tells you is the correct one.

If you can complete this or a similar process before you execute all your shots, you'll enjoy vastly better, more consistent performance.

Find Your Best Starting Move

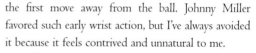

OVER THE YEARS, we've seen three basic techniques for starting the clubhead away from the ball. The move I prefer actually combines two of them.

Most golfers used to drag their hands away before the clubhead moved, to compensate for the twisting characteristics of wooden shafts. This can be seen in old photos of Bobby Jones's swing. However, this lagging-type action is unnecessary with modern shafts, and can produce inconsistency in swing plane and path if carried to extremes.

More common now is the opposite move: cocking or hinging the wrists very early in the takeaway, even as the first move away from the ball. Johnny Miller favored such early wrist action, but I've always avoided it because it feels contrived and unnatural to me.

The third way of starting back is what has become known as the "one-piece" takeaway. With this technique, the shaft and left arm remain in a straight line until the momentum of the swing causes the wrists to begin hinging about the time they pass hip height.

My preference lies halfway between the first and third techniques. I've played well at times when sensing a very slight lag as I initiate the takeaway, allowing me to feel the momentum of the clubhead beginning to swing. Essentially, however, I want everything from the clubhead to my left shoulder moving back together to promote consistency of path and plane.

I think most golfers will find my technique the most effective.

Start Back
Ridiculously Slowly

AFTER UNDER-CLUBBING and poor gripping, I believe beginning the swing too quickly does more to keep handicaps high than any other fault. Better players, too, are prone to it under pressure. The mental image I've used throughout my career when sensing that I'm starting the swing too quickly is that I'm going to make a terribly forced, ridiculously slow movement of the clubhead away from the ball.

To do that, it helps me most to picture all the active parts—clubhead, shaft, hands, arms, shoulders—moving back together, or in "one piece," for at least the first couple of feet of the backswing. I'm also sometimes helped by thinking of maintaining this super-slow tempo throughout the rest of the swing.

For a tighter focus on start-back tempo, visualize particularly your hands and arms moving away from the ball "ridiculously slowly." They won't actually do so, but mind-picturing them in slow motion is the best way I know to ensure an unhurried start to the swing.

SLOW

Paint a Picture for Perfect Tempo

TEMPO TO ME is the rate at which the club is swung back and then down through the ball. Because it's so related to mood and other mental and emotional factors, it's the hardest thing in golf to get right and keep right.

I like to use a large "picture" plus a "detail" from it when working on my tempo.

The complete canvas shows the entire backswing and downswing happening at the same pace or speed. Then, to give me a specific "feel" focal point during the swing, the detail image is of my hands doing the same thing.

The clubhead always travels much faster coming down than going back, and probably the hands do, too. But I play my best when I "see" my hands moving no faster swinging down than they did swinging back.

Smooth Your Takeaway with This Drill

IN LOOKING for an effective swing trigger, I've experimented mostly with the forward press—starting back by slightly inclining the hands toward the target—but with varying degrees of success.

The move I'd really like to use is the one you see here: setting the club in motion from a couple of feet ahead of the ball, rather than from directly behind it.

I've never quite had the nerve to try this in competition, but I do use it quite often in practice, applying that image of pace and flow to my regular takeaway. Nothing better sets me off on the correct plane and with all parts of my body working together.

Waltz Your Way to a Better Swing

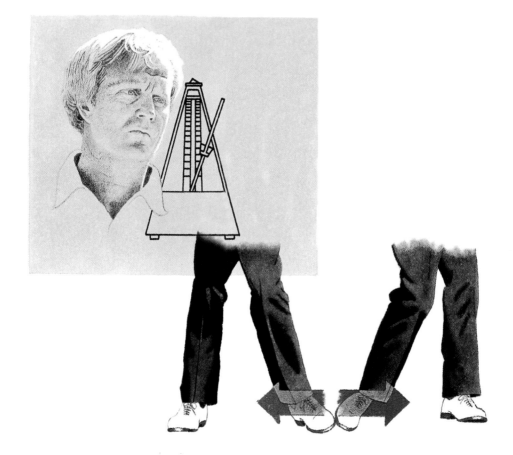

MATCHING YOUR FOOTWORK to a slow waltz tempo—one-two-three, one-two-three, one-two three—should help you improve your swing tempo. On the practice tee, narrow your stance and play some shots exaggerating the rocking motion of your feet. Begin with leisurely chip shot swings, timing your foot motion to the dance tempo. Swing without a club at first if that promotes smoother movement or better rhythm.

Once you have a feel for the moves, gradually extend the motion until you are using the amount of body action required for a full swing. The longer the swing, the more your left foot should roll inward on the backswing and your right foot should roll target-ward during the downswing.

If your heels want to come off the ground a little bit as the motion gets fuller, let them, but keep that good old one-two-three, one-two-three waltz tempo in your head throughout your practice sessions.

Visualize Razor Blade Wall for Inside Path

MANY SLICES AND PULLS originate from the clubhead traveling to the outside of the target line right from the start of the swing, in response to the hands moving incorrectly away from the body.

The feeling you want for about the first third of the backswing is that your hands remain the same distance from your torso as they were at address. That way, their path will match the plane of your upper-body turn, ensuring that the clubhead swings momentarily straight back along, and then progressively to the inside of, the target line.

To promote the proper action, I visualize a wall with razor blades tight up against the path my hands must initially follow. Now, if my hands get out of line, the penalty will be a long layoff from the game!

Swing Within Your Feet

ONE OF THE TOUGHEST CHALLENGES all golfers face is striking a balance between body motion and hand and arm action in the full swing.

It seems to me that, in general, golfers who've developed "good hands" through years of practice and play err toward too little use of the body. Conversely, less "trained" players try to make up for their lack of hand speed with excessive body action.

An image I've used to good effect in my game

whenever things seemed to be getting out of balance might help in both cases.

As you swing, picture yourself coiling and uncoiling so that no part of your torso moves beyond the confines of your feet. In other words, only your hands and arms move beyond the outer edge of your right foot on the backswing, and the same on the downswing in relation to your left foot.

Set Your Back Knee
Like a Sprinter's

LIKE A LOT OF BEGINNERS, I found it hard to coil correctly around my right leg on the backswing. The bigger the shoulder and hip turn I made, the more I tended to lose the knee flex I'd established at address.

When the right leg straightens going back, invariably it moves forward—rather than toward the target—starting down.

Eventually, my teacher, Jack Grout, hit on a piece of imagery that, with some hard practice, eliminated the fault.

What he told me was to visualize my right knee being in the same strongly flexed and springy condition at the completion of the backswing as that of a sprinter pushing off into a 100-meter dash.

It's a mind-picture I've long used in working on my foot and leg action.

Use Arm Pictures
for a Two-Sided Swing

GOLF TO ME is a two-sided game, but I've found that it helps to know, visualize, and mentally pre-program the role played by each side of the body. I do this chiefly by "seeing" and sensing the action of my hands and arms.

Contrary to earlier in my career, I've felt for some years that I control the pattern, tempo, and what I call the "texture" of the swing chiefly with my right hand and arm. This applies particularly to the motion away from the ball and the setting of the club at the top of the swing.

The role I "see" and sense my left hand and arm performing is simply that of a "spacer" and a support to establish, then sustain, an equal swing radius and arc throughout the action.

These images apply to my putting as well as my long game.

Similar "pictures" might help you better achieve the ideal balance between your right-side and left-side swing motions.

Let the Elbow Go

AS AN AMATEUR and young professional, I was frequently questioned about what some critics described as my "flying right elbow." A number of them actually forecast it would ultimately be my downfall as a player.

Whenever people criticized the position of my right elbow at the top of the backswing, I told them their eyes were deceiving them. If my elbow had pointed upward at the top—the classic "flying" position—I would have swung the club across the target line through impact and fought many recurring problems.

In reality, my elbow, although high, pointed directly behind me at the top, in keeping with my belief that the club must remain centered between the arms throughout the swing, just as it is at address. In addition, letting the elbow move away from my side was the only way I could achieve the upright plane and wide arc I wanted on all my full shots.

If you're lacking power, try letting your right elbow move freely away from your body on the backswing. As long as it points outward rather than upward at the top, this technique could help you gain substantial yardage.

Shove Your Butt Out
for a Better Turn

BECAUSE WE PLAY GOLF with the ball on the ground, we must incline our bodies to be able to swing the club through it. The angle of inclination is determined by physique combined with the shaft length of the club being used, and is established as part of our address posture.

A fundamental of good golf, and seemingly one of the hardest for less skilled players to achieve, is keeping the angle of inclination constant throughout the swing. Changing it, of course, disrupts the club-head arc, resulting in all kinds of miss-hits. If this is a problem for you, try an image that has helped me over the years. As you set up to the ball, shove your butt back and out as far as it will go, then visualize yourself keeping it there throughout the swing.

In addition to helping you retain your angles, thinking and sensing "butt stays back and out" will also create the bodily freedom to let you turn more fully and smoothly on both the backswing and through-swing.

Think Right Side for Correct Hip Action

BACK WHEN I was first learning golf, Jack Grout taught me that the correct hip action is rotational—the middle part of the body turning within its own space, like a revolving cylinder.

When I thought "turn left hip around," I would often slide laterally rather than coil and uncoil, with poor results in terms of both accuracy and distance. Eventually it struck me that, being right-handed, I might do better if I pictured the right hip rather than the left turning back and through.

It worked so well that I've used the image ever since whenever I need a hip-action thought.

Don't Force Your Torso Turn...

THE WORD "TURN" in golf refers to the coiling of the torso against the resistance of the lower body. Done correctly, the turn puts the club in position to approach the ball squarely and at high speed on the downswing.

Driving the ball far and straight, as I did at my peak and as Tiger Woods and other top players do now, certainly requires a full body turn, or coil, on the backswing. However, many golfers become overly conscious of turning and try to force the shoulders around as an independent action. Instead, the coiling of the torso should simply be a response to the free, full swinging of the club with the hands and arms from the moment the backswing begins. High-speed photography proves this point by showing that the clubhead is the first thing to move in all of the best golf swings.

A full turn is a good objective, but let the swinging of the hands, arms, and club lead the way. In other words, the turn is a subconscious result of the swinging motion, not a forced effort in itself.

...But Extend Those Arms Fully

THE GOLF SWING is easiest for me when I get my hands fully underneath the shaft of the club at the top of the backswing. I hit the ball farthest and straightest when I fully extend my arms during the swing.

Look at the highlighted area of the larger illustration and you'll note that the upper part of my right arm is still higher than the upper part of my left arm—even at this fairly advanced stage of the backswing.

Trying to replicate this position could help you greatly if you have trouble either positioning your hands correctly at the top or achieving full arm extension, or both. Feeling that the clubface turns slightly under as you start back, and that your hands stay slightly inside the arc of the clubhead all the way to the top, will help you make the move. Note the "slightly" in both cases.

Our Nicklaus/Flick Golf School teachers encountered many fairly good golfers who tried to get the toe of the club up in the air quickly, or their hands underneath the shaft, or both, by rotating the clubface open or clockwise right off the ball. Invariably, this produced too flat a swing plane, too cramped an arm swing, and incorrect hands positioning to the side of the club at the top.

The right-arm-above-left thought and move is the best way I know to fix such faults.

Build Maximum Spring into Your Swing

ONE OF MY GOALS in working on my full swing is to produce a sense of springiness in my body as everything changes direction. Particularly, I want the feeling that I've "gathered" myself sufficiently at the top so that my weight springs from my right to my left side, followed by my upper body springing from a low to a high position as it reacts to the uncoiling down below.

When these feelings are elusive, an image I like to use is that of a pitcher firing a baseball.

As the torso and arms wind up, the right knee flexes and braces, the weight shifts hard back onto the right heel, the hips coil around tighter and tighter, then—POW!—the spring is released and the ball rockets to the catcher.

If your shots lack zip, throw a couple of golf balls down the driving range, then try for the same feel in your swing.

Make a Smooth Transition

ONE OF THE QUESTIONS I've been asked most frequently at clinics over the years is whether a golfer should pause at the top of the backswing. My answer has always been a qualified "no."

The reason nothing comes to a discernible stop in most fine swings is that the forward motion begins as a reflexive or involuntary reaction to the backward motion before it actually has been completed. See the illustration for the mechanics, noting how the release of the torque created between my upper and lower body (left) initiates the uncoiling of my hips before my wrists have completed their hinging (right).

Why, then, a qualified "no"?

Rushing the transition from backward to forward motions is just as destructive as deliberately pausing between the two. That's why one of my key swing thoughts over the years has been, "Start down no faster than you begin swinging back."

Move Body Around– Not Forward–at Impact

YOU WILL NEVER hit the ball consistently long and straight if you slide or sway your hips significantly toward the target on the downswing.

In the best swings, the forward shifting or shuttling of the knees that initiates the downswing causes the hips to move laterally before they begin unwinding, or "clearing." But that lateral motion is always slight compared to the hip rotation that quickly follows it.

The simplest way I know to achieve the correct balance of lateral and rotational hip motion is to not allow your left hip to get ahead of your left foot at any point in the downswing or follow-through. In other words, the body action is mostly "around," not forward, through the strike.

If you find these moves difficult to achieve, focus on keeping your head behind the ball until the shot is well on its way. This will encourage you to turn, rather than slide your body through for solid, powerful contact.

Pull the Clubhead Through

GOOD GOLF SHOTS result from delivering the clubhead to the ball when the clubhead is traveling either from slightly inside or directly along the target line, with the face looking squarely at the target.

Such delivery is impossible if the clubface gets ahead of the hands before impact. That's why, in my mind's eye, I like to "see" my hands leading the clubhead slightly as the ball is struck.

Setting up with the left arm and clubshaft in a straight line from the left shoulder to the ball promotes such impact "geometry." So does a sense that the club is being pulled through impact with the left side, rather than thrown through with the right side.

Restore the Radius for Proper "Release"

THE Q AND A sessions at my clinics indicate many golfers have a poor understanding of the downswing action denoted by the word "release."

Here are a couple of images that have helped me a lot over the years and should clear up the mystery.

Imagine yourself standing at address inside a circle centered at the extremity of your left shoulder and passing through the middle of the ball. Your left arm and the club's shaft form a radius of that circle. When they return to exactly the same relationship at impact—when, so to speak, you fully "restore the radius"—you are releasing correctly and completely.

Here's an even simpler aid to a proper release: Visualize extending the clubhead at impact as far away from you as it can possibly go. Just make sure you retain the body angles established by your address posture.

Think "Toe" for a Controlled Fade

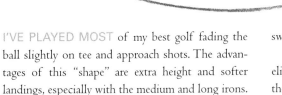

I'VE PLAYED MOST of my best golf fading the ball slightly on tee and approach shots. The advantages of this "shape" are extra height and softer landings, especially with the medium and long irons.

I pre-program the fade at address: body aligned a little left of target for an out-to-in swing path; clubface aimed a little right of target to set up the slightly oblique hit that produces a touch of left-to-right sidespin. Then I switch in a mind-picture that virtually guarantees the same swing path/clubface relationship at impact.

This image is of the toe of the club always traveling in a greater arc than its heel. In other words, as the club swings back the toe moves progressively farther away from the body than the heel; then, coming down, the toe never quite catches up with the heel until after impact.

The beauty of this image is that it allows me to hit the ball hard without fear of pulling it straight left, always a big concern for faders.

Sweep Long-Irons with Your Driver Swing

THERE WAS A TIME when I had more confidence with a 1- or 2-iron than I did with a 9-iron or pitching wedge.

One of the reasons was an ability to sweep the ball off the grass with the long-irons, catching it just a fraction of an inch before the clubhead reached the lowest point of the swing.

Two images helped me achieve that type of action. The first was to visualize myself reproducing the same kind of wide, full swing I made with the driver as I set up to the shot. The second was then to forget all about the ball and picture myself nipping the top off the grass directly beneath it.

Try these images if you suffer from the common fault of trying to make a long-iron shot go up in the air by hitting steeply down into the ball.

Always "Feel" that Clubhead

OVER THE YEARS, the better I've been able to feel the weight of the clubhead against the tension of the shaft during the swing, the better I've generally played.

This sensation is most critical at two points: the end of the backswing and the start of the downswing. As the club approaches the top, I like to feel that the clubhead's weight is pulling my arms and hands into their top-of-the-swing positions. Starting down, I try to sense the clubhead lagging until the downswing has been initiated by my feet and legs, at which point I know I can safely "release" with my hands and arms.

Proper tempo—making all the movements of the swing in an unhurried and rhythmical sequence—is a big factor in achieving these sensations. When my tempo is smooth, the swing feels easy and my confidence soars; I know I will pull off many more shots than I will miss.

Pay Attention to Your Follow-Through

OBVIOUSLY, nothing you do after the ball leaves the clubface is going to influence its behavior. Nevertheless, paying attention to your follow-through can be more helpful than you might imagine.

The three elements to focus on are your hands, right shoulder, and head. The higher your hands finish, the farther along the target line they and the clubhead will have swung after impact. This is a key contributor to accuracy. Hands finishing past and below the left shoulder indicate an overly flat swing and/or excessive wrist-roll through impact. You should seek the feeling of your right shoulder moving down and dropping lower than your left shoulder during the early part of follow-through, indicating that you have hit directly through the ball with full power.

Until the completion of the follow-through pulls your head up and around, it should remain in its original address position, but with enough targetward tilt to let you watch the ball's initial flight out of the corner of your left eye. This signifies a steady head through impact—my lifelong number-one swing fundamental.

Understand the "Release"

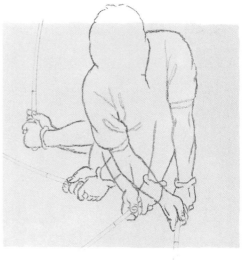

THE BETTER YOUR "RELEASE," the more powerfully and accurately you will strike the ball. So what exactly is the "release"? Stated as simply as possible: a free, full, and fast swinging of the clubhead through the ball by the hands, wrists, and arms at the appropriate time during the downswing.

I believe that, as long as the downswing is initiated with the feet and legs, it is impossible to begin releasing too early. There is, however, a proviso to this rule. In making a conscious effort to start down from the ground up, many golfers overdo lower-body action, to the point of forcing their hips too far toward of the target before they begin uncoiling. Releasing fully after a hip slide is extremely difficult, if not impossible.

Study the best players and you will see that their left hip never moves forward of the ball during the downswing. Not allowing yours to do so is critical to releasing as freely, fully, and speedily as you are capable of doing.

Live with Shorter But Not with Faster

AS A YOUNGSTER, my teacher, Jack Grout, tried to get me to swing as fully as possible—not just because he wanted me to hit the ball as hard and far as possible from day one, but also because he knew that, just like every other golfer, my swing would shorten with age.

Jack was right on both counts. But, as the years passed, he and I worried less about the size of my swing and more about its pace and tempo—that I still gave myself sufficient time within the framework of the more compact action to complete all the motions necessary to strike the ball accurately and forcefully.

On occasion, I've attempted to re-lengthen my swing, but the end result always felt so unnatural that it would never work in competition. Thus I continue to focus on avoiding the fault that so frequently accompanies time-induced swing shortening—excessively speeding everything up.

From what I see in my travels, others might benefit from a similar strategy as the years roll by.

Encourage Your Kids to "Whale" It

GOLF TEACHING HAS become a lot more positional and mechanical since my youth, which probably is okay for established players seeking to fine-tune their games or raise their shot-making capabilities to higher levels.

But, when it comes to teaching children, I still believe the strategy taught me by Jack Grout and to Arnold Palmer by his father, Deacon, is the best.

Jack and Deacon wanted Arnie and me to swing as hard as possible from day one, and to heck with where the ball went.

There were four reasons for this. First was that most kids enjoy golf more when they're allowed to "whale" away at the ball. Second, the harder we swung, the faster we'd build golf muscles. Third, distance is a huge competitive asset, once a golfer learns to control it. Finally, it's much easier to learn to control power once you've developed it than it is to develop power once you've learned control.

Naturally, I adopted that philosophy with my own children, and am glad to say that it seems to have worked. All five of them are able to hit it a ton. The ones who have really taken to the game have become steadily better at control as consciousness of scoring gradually replaced their "smash it" instincts.

Try My Lifelong Full-Swing Basics

MASTERING THE BASICS of the golf swing is crucial to building a reliable game. With all the theories out there these days on how to swing, it's tempting to change your focus every time you hear something new. Try not to do that. Until you have a handle on swing basics, you shouldn't wander into unfamiliar territory. Here are the fundamentals that have served me throughout my career:

- A steady, if not stationary, head throughout the swing, with the eyes on the ball until after impact.
- A smooth tempo, particularly at the start of the swing and during the transition from backswing to through-swing.
- Free-swinging arms, back and through.
- A complete, torque-creating backswing that coils the upper body against the resistance of the lower body.
- An initiation of the through-swing from the ground up: The feet, knees, and hips lead the shoulders, arms, hands, and clubhead.
- A complete release of the clubhead through the ball.
- A full and perfectly balanced follow-through position.

This list is not to suggest that I've worked on these points simultaneously throughout my career, only that they collectively have been my primary areas of focus. Any good teaching pro would be delighted to flesh out these factors with you, with the emphasis targeted to your level of ability.

POWER

FOR MOST PLAYERS, the most enjoyable and sought-after moments in golf come from hitting the ball as long as they can—and particularly off the tee.

As much as I enjoyed the advantage I held with my youthful power, I found myself tempering it increasingly over the years, as experience taught me that distance in the wrong direction is usually penalizing. That's why, if you watched me at my peak, you might have noticed a great many 3-wood or long-iron tee shots, because of the premium I placed on position and not power. Course management is about putting the ball in a position that leaves you the best possible next shot. Playing smart sometimes means sacrificing power and your ego.

If faced with a long par 4 or par 5, with a wide fairway and minimal trouble, by all means, give it a whack. But when the landing areas narrow, the situations become dangerously tight, and the trouble ahead increases, winning golf becomes much more a game of precision than one of power.

Remember: golf offers no bonus points for distance. In this game, the only numbers that count are those on the scorecard.

Get Your Tee Height Right

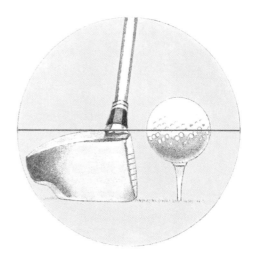

HOW HIGH SHOULD YOU TEE the ball for the driver? Too basic to bother with? Don't you believe it!

You'll get the most out of your driver when it meets the ball traveling slightly above the grass and either exactly at the bottom of its arc or just at the beginning of the upswing. Such impact is most easily achieved when about half the ball shows above the top edge of the driver and its bottom rests lightly on the ground.

Hitting into the wind, the common wisdom is to tee the ball lower to promote a lower, more boring flight. The problem with that is, the lower the ball is teed, the greater the risk of swinging down into it too steeply, thereby imparting extra backspin that costs distance by increasing the height of the shot and decreasing its roll. Also, the lower the ball is teed, the greater the danger of catching the ground before impact. This suggests teeing lower only if you are skilled enough to still deliver the driver solidly into the back of the ball at a low angle without hitting it fat. Most golfers will be better off teeing normally and striking the ball solidly.

Should you tee higher in a tailwind? Once again, the answer depends on your skill level. Always make solid contact your top goal.

The physics of the game suggest it's easier to fade drives by teeing the ball low, and to draw them by teeing high, but fine swing control and high confidence are usually necessary to finesse shots that way.

Look to Your Feet to Plug Power Leak

FOOT ACTION may not seem like much of a contributor to good golf compared to all the bigger, bolder, more intriguing motions going on up above. But, for a real insight to its importance, see how much power you can pour into a shot while keeping your feet absolutely still. You'll be lucky

to hit the ball out of your shadow.

As time has passed, I've noticed more and more that when I fail to let my feet dictate both the pace and flow of my swing, I'm headed for serious power leakage. When my feet don't work well, neither do my legs and hips—the key creators of the leverage that generates centrifugal force, which delivers the clubhead to the ball at high speed.

The fix in my case lies in making my feet leaders rather than followers, especially as I change direction from backswing to downswing. Even as the backward momentum of the clubhead is completing my wrist-cock, I want to feel my left heel solidly replanting itself as both ankles roll sharply target-ward, first pulling my knees along with them, then forcefully unwinding my hips to make room for my arms to swing freely past my body.

If you're suffering a power leak, try this feet-as-leaders flow of motion. It might be just the plug you need.

Open Your Back Foot for More Windup

HAVE YOU EVER heard a golfer blame his rear foot for a mis-hit? The fact that you almost certainly haven't does not mean that its role in shotmaking is unimportant.

For normal shots, the ideal positioning of the rear foot is either square to the target line or slightly toed out. This promotes a low takeaway along the target line for the first several inches and sound lower-body action starting down.

When seeking to hit the ball longer and higher, however, a small adjustment in this area can be a big help, in two ways:

Angling the back foot farther away from the target line promotes a fuller and more powerful upper-body coil going back, while preserving balance. On the downswing, it helps keep the body behind the ball, promoting a shallow, sweeping impact that results in solidly struck, longer shots.

Experiment during practice to discover the exact alignment that works best for you.

Adjust Your Left Foot for Stronger Uncoil

EXPERIMENTING with your stance could give you more distance, particularly with your driver.

For instance, at my peak I hit most powerfully when I turned my left foot out at about a 45-degree angle, combined with moving my right foot forward to give me a slightly open stance. The reason was that these two small adjustments let me uncoil my hips faster on the downswing, thereby clearing my body out of the way for my arms and hands to deliver the clubhead to the ball as freely and forcefully as possible.

Other stance variations that can produce more distance include turning out the right foot more than normal to facilitate more backswing body coiling and pulling the right foot back to produce a draw-inducing closed stance.

Stick with proven fundamentals in the big elements of technique, but don't be afraid to experiment with minor nuances to discover what works best for you.

Make Your Arc Wide, Wide, Wide

THE BIGGER THE ARC the clubhead travels during the swing—assuming, of course, that its passage is well controlled—the farther the ball flies.

For me, creating a large arc has always depended on extending the clubhead fully away from my body in the first part of the backswing, then extending it fully again as it "chases" the ball after impact.

Among the best images I've come up with for doing both was one that helped me win a fourth U.S. Open at Baltusrol in 1980. Swinging back, I visualized my arms moving as far away from my body as they would go without my head accompanying them. Swinging through, I pictured them extending as far toward the target as they would reach without any forward head movement. I've rarely hit the ball longer with less sense of effort.

Wedge a Ball to Coil Your Spring Tighter

IT'S HARD TO PLAY WELL if your right knee—left for southpaws—straightens, buckles, or becomes otherwise unstable during the backswing. Such movement changes the arc or plane of the swing, making it difficult to accurately deliver the clubhead to the ball.

Jack Grout

Even worse, an unstable right knee greatly diminishes the amount of power-producing torque you can achieve between the upper body and lower body.

One quick fix for this problem is simply to set the majority of your weight on the inside of your right foot at address, and keep it there throughout the backswing. During my early days, my teacher, Jack Grout, took that idea a step further and had me wedge a golf ball under the outside part of my right foot, canting the foot and knee inward and virtually "locking" them there for the backswing.

Using this drill, it took me only a short time to sense the feeling of truly "coiling the spring" while going back, as well as maintaining the correct arc and plane. Much of this was due to a flexed, stable right knee. Give Jack's drill a try if you suspect your knee action is costing you distance or consistency.

Anchor Yourself

I'VE ALWAYS HAD a full swing arc and big body turn going back, but those elements alone never made me a long hitter. The key to a powerful backswing is creating torque, whereby the upper body winds against the lower body to create a coil that unloads on the downswing. For me, the best way to ensure a good coil is to key on the "anchors" in my swing.

My upper-body anchor is the back of my neck (inset); it should stay in the same place throughout the backswing. Any movement up, down, or sideways as I swing the club back diminishes the amount of torque I can generate.

My lower-body anchors are my feet; I always keep my weight on the insides of my feet. As I turn back, my weight rolls from the inside of my left foot onto the inside of my right, and then reverses direction on the downswing. Weight drifting to the outside of the right foot on the backswing is a sure sign that you're not "winding the spring."

To make sure you're getting the most out of your swing, check your anchors. Remember, you need to maximize torque going back if you want maximum power at impact.

Drive the Ball Forward, Not Down

YOU'LL HIT YOUR BEST DRIVES when the clubhead is traveling either precisely parallel to the ground or slightly upward at impact. That's because the ball is hit forcefully forward, which is imperative to achieving optimum trajectory and maximum distance.

Your worst drives usually occur when you deliver the clubhead on an oblique or downward angle, imparting a glancing blow and excessive backspin on the ball at the cost of forward thrust. Weak, sliced pop-ups result from the most extreme form of this fault.

Here are several keys to ensuring a sweeping, or shallow, delivery of the clubhead through impact:

• Tee the ball so at least half of it is higher than the top edge of the clubface;

• Position the ball no farther back than an inch or so behind your left instep;

• Be sure your hands at address are no farther forward than the center of your left thigh;

• Set your head behind the ball at address, then keep it there through impact;

• Make sure your left hip never passes your left foot on the forward swing, ensuring the full clearance of your left side and a complete release of the clubhead with the hands, wrists, and arms.

Get these positions right and you'll transfer maximum energy to the ball at impact and hit your tee shots farther than ever.

Strike Squarely for Maximizing Distance

MOST GOLFERS seeking extra distance focus mainly on increasing clubhead speed. But many would enjoy better results by working on the other factors that govern shot distance: hitting the ball squarely and making contact on the middle of the clubface.

How important are these factors? Check out the players on the LPGA Tour. Few possess the strength of the average male amateur, but most hit the ball farther than they do. This indicates that LPGA players have better coordination and control, which enables them to deliver the clubhead to the ball more squarely and accurately, even through it may not be traveling as fast.

For another reason, consider that each of us has an innate maximum when it comes to controllable clubhead speed—determined by physique and conditioning—but none of us has a built-in limit on how much more precisely we can swing the club—particularly with the help of a capable and caring teacher. So, set your sights on hitting the ball more purely to maximize your power, without swinging out of control.

Swing Through, Not To, the Ball

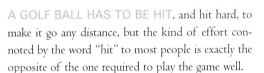

A GOLF BALL HAS TO BE HIT, and hit hard, to make it go any distance, but the kind of effort connoted by the word "hit" to most people is exactly the opposite of the one required to play the game well.

The reason, of course, is that "hit" suggests to so many of us a violent application of the body. What sending a golf ball far and true demands is speedy application of the clubhead.

The best mind-picture I've come across for turning force into speed—or strength into quickness—is the simplest one: Swing the clubhead through, not to, the ball.

The image of the ball simply getting in the way of the clubhead at some point during its swinging motion is as old as golf itself. What that indicates to me is that nobody has been able to come up with a better one.

Hit Hard with the Clubhead

READ THAT TITLE AGAIN. Does it sound like I'm stating the obvious? Well, particularly when going through a bad spell, it's all too easy to become so immersed in "swing mechanics" that you forget the object of the exercise—to hit the ball the maximum distance and with good direction. And, since you don't strike the ball with anything but the clubhead, stay focused on the basic motion of swinging the clubhead freely through the ball.

Here's how I try to make sure I do that. Given a sound, torque-producing backswing, my downswing is initiated reflexively from the ground up by my weight shifting to my left foot as my knees shuttle toward the target and my hips begin to unwind.

Once that's happening, I want my arms and hands to swing the clubhead through the ball as fast and forcefully as they possibly can—with the single proviso that they follow, rather than lead, my lower-body actions.

If I get that sequence right, no matter how hard I swing, I never "release too early," "come over the top," or commit other common downswing sins. Remember, the sequence occurs from the ground up—feet, knees, hips, and shoulders, then moves to the arms, hands, and clubhead. That's the key to solid, consistent ball-striking.

FAULTS AND FIXES

BEN HOGAN AND LEE TREVINO are two of the greatest ball-strikers our game has ever seen, yet even they suffered occasional flaws or fluctuations in form. That's because no one ever has been able to make himself or herself into a golfing machine, and no one ever will. After all, golf is a lifetime pursuit of problem-solving, and that is perhaps one of the beauties of the game.

When I had a problem to solve, I began the process by first sitting down and trying to figure out by myself exactly what I was doing wrong. I did this by breaking down the game and the swing to its simplest cause-and-effect terms. Invariably, I began with the grip and the set-up, relating everything back to the way my shots behaved, and particularly the direction in which the ball started and the shape or curvature of the shot.

Secondly, I would put whatever potential solution I came up with to the test on the practice tee or green. If it didn't work, I would discard the idea quickly, so as not to waste time and energy. Then, I'd think more about the problem and possible solutions, and repeat the physical trial.

During my most successful years, I knew my game well enough to be able to self-correct my flaws much of the time. When I failed, Jack Grout's phone would inevitably ring.

Think "Deep" to Fight "Steep"

DETERMINED TO AVOID A REPETITION after playing poorly in 1979, I spent much of the early part of 1980 working on a full-swing change that both my teacher, Jack Grout, and I had decided was overdue.

Always favoring an upright plane, I had allowed my shoulder turn and arm swing to become excessively steep, to the point of losing both power and accuracy.

The mind-pictures that eventually got my shoulders turning more and tilting less, and my arms swinging less upward and farther behind me, derived from the word "deep."

"Deep" continues to help me, both in practice and, when added to a "complete-the-backswing" thought, during competition.

Try thinking "deep" if you're having difficulty applying the club solidly to the back of the ball on a regular basis.

Use Mind-Pictures
to Cultivate Draw

BECAUSE FADING SHOTS from left to right has been the easiest and most natural technique for me, I've always needed strong mind-pictures to draw the ball from right to left. Here are a couple that have helped a lot over the years:

If I were standing outside myself looking down the target line, I would see my right shoulder moving very much "underneath" my left shoulder as my hands swing to the ball from inside the target line, then on to a big, high finish.

If I had no golf club in my hands as I made that move, I would look just like a softball pitcher throwing underhand toward home plate.

Lighten Grip Pressure to Cure a Slice

HERE IS A TIP that's especially good for seniors, but applicable to everyone. If you're aiming the club-face and aligning your body square to your target, and your shots still slice badly from left to right, check your grip pressure.

Too tight a hold—particularly with the right hand—prevents a complete release of the clubhead through impact, which leaves the face open.

An overly tight grip also promotes out-and-over shoulder action at the start of the downswing, which delivers the clubhead to the ball from out to in across the target line.

Young or old, you could be happily surprised by how much curve a lighter grip takes out of your shots.

Use Clubface Images to Help "Work" Shots

DO YOU FIND IT DIFFICULT to draw or fade shots, even after making the necessary set-up adjustments? Try the clubface images that have helped me "work" the ball throughout my career.

As long as you swing the way you set up, aligning your shoulders right of target (below) and closing the face slightly at address should assure that the ball starts a little right of target and curves gently back to it.

For "insurance," visualize the toe of the club overtaking the heel through impact (below right)

and continuing to move farther ahead as the follow-through deepens.

Reverse the process to fade shots. Begin by aligning your shoulders a little left of target and opening the clubface slightly. Then "see" and feel the heel of the club always staying ahead of, or leading, the toe through impact (below left). Translate that image into feel with a few practice swings. Keeping your right hand "under" your left through impact will help you do so.

Fix the "Fats"

HITTING THE GROUND behind the ball is known as hitting "fat" or "chunking." It's a common fault among high handicappers but can afflict better players at times. Either way, it's a sure score-wrecker.

Numerous swing faults can provoke the problem, but I believe the most frequent cause is one of the easiest to fix: excessive head movement.

Common sense tells us that changing our head position during the swing alters the arc the clubhead is traveling along. Thus, one way to almost guarantee a fat hit is to dip the head during the downswing, thereby lowering the path of the descending clubhead. Swaying the head to the right during the backswing can also cause the fault, by shifting the point where the swing bottoms out to a spot behind the ball.

If you hit more than the occasional fat shot, look to your head before tampering with other swing elements. The likelihood is that keeping your head a little steadier is all the fix you need.

For a Steady Head, Imagine a Wheel

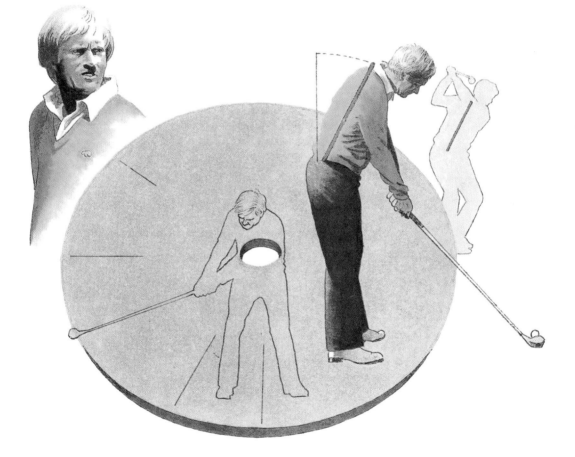

MOVE YOUR HEAD too much during the swing and the accompanying change in clubhead arc almost guarantees a miss-hit. Keep your head too still and your action becomes weak and wooden.

A possible solution lies in an image of mine that allows the head to behave as it should without conscious direction.

Imagine the arc the clubhead describes as the rim of a wheel, your torso as the hub, and your spine as the axle within the hub.

As you swing, keep the axle in place as you rotate the hub smoothly around it, thereby also rotating the rim.

By leaning toward the ball from the waist as you address it, you incline the axle in that direction.

Try to retain its angle of inclination throughout the entire swing.

Move the Ball Back to Beat Pulling

THE PULLED SHOT is one of a few poor shots that feel pretty solid. With the pull, the clubface is square to an out-to-in swing path at impact, resulting in a straight ball flight left of the target (for right-handed golfers). Since the ball doesn't curve, as it does with a hook or a slice, it might not look too bad either. The problem is it ends up way left of your target.

Since the pull results from an out-to-in swing path, it can often be attributed to positioning the ball too far forward in the stance at address. This being the case, the clubhead is already moving inside the target line when it reaches impact. Make sure you set up with the ball no farther forward than the inside of your left heel. If you continue to fight the pull, try moving the ball back little by little until your ball flight straightens out.

Keep in mind also that swinging the clubhead out toward the target after impact and completing the follow-through with your hands high will reduce the risk of pulling.

Diagnose with Divots and Ball Flight

ONE OF THE HARD THINGS about the game of golf is our inability to see ourselves in action. That's why we need to take advantage of all available clues.

The direction of your divots is a clear indicator of what you are doing with the club, and even more so is the ball's flight.

A divot mark cutting from right to left relative to your target line is the result of an out-to-in swing path. This path produces pulled shots when the clubface alignment matches it, or a left-to-right slice when the clubface is open to it at impact.

The opposite divot mark shape, from left to right relative to your target line, indicates an in-to-out swing path. This causes a push when the clubface alignment matches the path, or a right-to-left hook when the clubface points left of it at impact.

Knowing what you are doing with the club at impact is key to playing your best golf. Your divot marks, combined with the ball's flight pattern, are sound indicators.

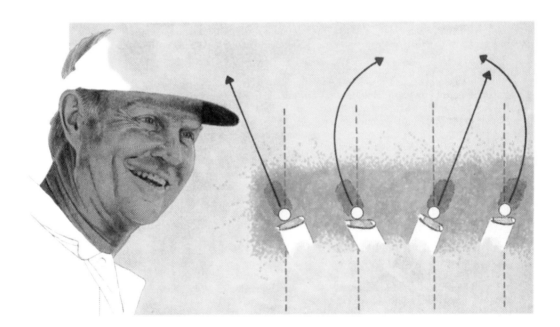

Stop Being a "Loser"

"LOSING" THE CLUB at the top of the back-swing is one of golf's most common errors, costing the golfer both accuracy and power. The fault gener-ally derives from loosening the fingers of the left hand, thereby allowing the clubhead to flop around like a wet noodle. Such loss of control frequently comes from swinging back so fast that the fingers aren't strong enough to secure the club as it reaches the top.

Try the following if you suspect you're a "loser":

Keep your grip on the club soft while setting up for the swing. Firm up your hands only a millisec-ond before you begin the backswing. It might help you to think of this firming as your swing trigger, as I do. You might also consider substituting a for-ward press instead of the firming, as I also do.

Next, initiate your swing as smoothly and slowly as you possibly can, even to the point of visualizing a slow-motion start. Be sure, however, not to further tighten your hands as you do so—increasing grip pressure is as destructive as easing it.

Finally, don't try to consciously cock your wrists. Simply allow the ever-increasing momentum of the clubhead to hinge them reflexively.

104

Beware of "Flash Speed"

MANY TIMES after a good golfer pulls or pull-hooks a shot, he'll say to himself, "I swung over the top." In other words, he diagnoses the fault as shoving or throwing the club onto an out-to-in path during the downswing, usually as a result of faulty body action.

Working with teacher Rick Smith, I discovered that these left-finishing shots are sometimes the result of a very different kind of downswing glitch—neatly defined by Rick as "flash speed."

Flash speed occurs when, instead of rerouting his downswing plane forward or to the outside of the target line, as in "over the top," the golfer drops his club excessively rearward or to the inside on the way down. Sensing that he will now have difficulty "finding the ball"—delivering the clubface to it correctly—he overworks his hands and wrists, usually with a flipping action that causes the clubface to close too quickly. Alternatively, after "flashing" some shots left, he'll hang on too long with his hands and wrists, pushing the ball to the right.

Understanding and then guarding against these moves greatly helped both my son Gary and me as we worked on our games for the 1993 season.

The antidote to flash speed, of course, is to swing the club down on a plane that complements your backswing plane, rather than rerouting it in an effort to swing excessively from the inside.

When a Problem Arises, Get to Its Root

ONE OF THE WORST PUTTS I've ever hit was at the 17th hole in the final round of the 1966 Masters. I eventually won the tournament in a play-off, but would have done so in regulation if I'd made that three-footer. I aimed the ball at the right corner of the hole and hit it firmly, but pulled it so badly that it never came close.

The natural reaction to this kind of situation is to assume that your nerves failed you and to try to put the matter aside, but I knew better. There was a mechanical reason why I missed that putt. What made me certain were the 38 putts I'd required two days previously, seven of them from less than five feet. My problem was identifying the flaw.

Television came to the rescue as I watched a replay of that awful miss at the 17th on Sunday. My head was too far out over the target line, forcing me to look back or inward at the ball. This meant that, although I felt like I was squaring the putter face correctly, I was actually aiming it to the left of where I wanted to start the ball rolling. After practicing for a while that evening with my head correctly positioned, I did not hit a single poor putt in Monday's playoff.

Moral #1: When your game goes bad, be sure to get to the real root of the problem. Moral #2: In matters of alignment, trust a camera, teacher, or knowledgeable friend's reading more than your own feel.

THE SHORT GAME
AND SPECIAL SHOTS

FOR MOST OF MY EARLY CAREER, I was strong enough to hit most greens in regulation or better, even from heavy rough. And, once on the green, I had a great deal of confidence in my putting, especially inside 10 feet. Consequently, in those days I didn't pay enough attention to the critical aspects that make up the short game—chipping, pitching, and bunker play.

My mindset changed as I grew older and matured as a golfer. Once I began to work much harder at my game around the greens, as well as what we call "recovery shots," I gained an additional confidence that countered any drop-off in strength. When this newfound ability contributed greatly to victories on the Senior PGA Tour, I realized what I might I have missed in my youth.

Tiger Woods is considered today's most complete golfer—and arguably the most complete player in the game's history—due in large part to his determination to put in as much work on his game around the greens as he has on his game from tee to green. I've never been one to look back, but, knowing what I do now about the importance of chipping, pitching, bunker play, and possessing a repertoire of recovery shots, one can't help but wonder, "What if?"

Choose the Correct Chip

SUCCESS AROUND THE GREEN depends as much on good decision-making as it does on good technique. For instance, once I decide to play a chip shot, I have three types of chips from which to choose: the basic chip, the backspin chip, and the runner. Picking the right one for the situation at hand dramatically increases my chances for success.

When ground and course conditions are normal, I play the basic chip, guiding the club back and through with my left hand and letting my right provide the hit, with no rolling of the wrists. When I need a softer shot with some bite, I choose the backspin chip, opening the clubface slightly at address and trying to cut across the ball from out to in to impart backspin. And when I have a lot of green to work with, I use the runner, in which I swing from in to out through impact, rolling my wrists over and applying hook-spin to the ball.

Try these shots for yourself, and develop a feel for when and how to use them on the course. Remember, learning to pick the right chip is just as important as mastering the technique.

Think of Limber Shaft for Chipping Consistently

ROLLING THE BALL at a consistent speed is a great aid to chipping it close to the hole every time. Consistency of roll depends for me on swinging at a uniform tempo, accommodating the distance variations by the degree of loft I select.

As in putting, the image I use to keep my chipping tempo slow, smooth, and soft is of a limber shaft, only this time of about double the firmness I visualize on the greens.

Now, if I swing back too fast, the clubhead will lag behind my hands. If my backswing pace is good but I quicken up coming down, my hands will drag the clubhead through the ball. If I get lazy or hesitant coming down, the clubhead will swing into the ball ahead of my hands.

My tempo is right on the nose when the clubhead and my hands maintain a consistent relationship throughout the action—or, to put it another way, when the shaft never "bends."

Use Your Left Arm to Firm Up Your Pitching

THE WEAKEST PART of my game during my best years was always wedge play—pitching the ball from about 100 yards and in. It cost me a couple of majors, and more regular tournaments than I care to think about.

A big contributor to the problem was a tendency to be insufficiently firm in my left arm, with the result that the width of my swing arc varied, usually being too narrow. This produced a variance in both distance and direction that was highly frustrating.

When I finally identified my left arm as the culprit, I began to concentrate on it during the swing, seeking the feeling that I was keeping it firm and straight throughout the entire action. This alone produced improvement, but I began to pitch the ball even better when the firm, straight left arm allowed

me to improve my timing by starting the downswing at the same speed I completed the backswing.

If your pitch shots are inconsistent, give my medicine a try. If thinking "firm" produces too stilted or wooden an action, replace it with "straight"—or whatever thought it takes to keep your leading and controlling arm swinging on the same path back and through.

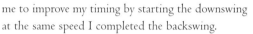

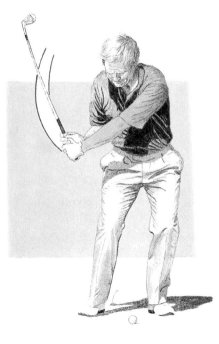

"Toss a Softball" to Beat Scooping Motion

THERE'S A TENDENCY in pitching, particularly when playing less than a full shot, to be fearful of applying the clubhead to the ball with sufficient aggressiveness.

The fault usually stems from holding back with the right side, to the point where the action becomes a shoving or scooping motion, rather than a firm, crisp release of the clubhead through the ball.

One time when I was struggling with my wedge play during my early days, my teacher, Jack Grout, demonstrated how the motion of the right arm in bowling, and also in pitching a softball, very closely resembles that of the right arm in a golf swing. Ever since, I've found that picturing myself making those other sports motions helps me to properly release my right arm and the clubhead through the ball when playing pitch shots.

"Seeing" and sensing those moves might also help you get the ball closer to the pin more often with your short-irons and wedges.

Try the Pitch-and-Run

LIKE MANY SENIORS, the passage of time has forced me to work harder on my short game to make up for decreasing length. One of the shots I've come to value more as I've gotten better at it is the pitch-and-run.

Shooting at the flagstick and "sticking" the ball with the wedges is fine when you are in top form but costly when you're not. I think you'll find that pitching-and-running the ball is equally effective on good swings and produces better results on poor ones. The shot is particularly useful in windy conditions, on fast greens, and on relatively flat courses.

You can play a pitch-and-run with a wedge by closing the face and positioning the ball well back in your stance, but the shot is more easily executed with the 7-, 8-, or 9-iron, depending upon the required amount of roll.

For better control, grip down on the club an inch or two, then set up with a narrow stance, weight favoring the left side, the ball in the middle of your stance, and your hands set ahead of the ball. I play the shot best with a short, crisp stroke in which the clubface never catches up with my left hand as I swing through the ball.

Until you've practiced this shot sufficiently to acquire feel for flight relative to roll, it's probably wise to hit a little harder than you think necessary, on the principle that you'll be short more often than long.

Work "Right Palm Under" for Soft Lobs

THE KEY TO PLAYING high, floating, soft-landing shots—such as a gentle lob over a bunker to a tight pin position—is keeping the clubface open through impact and well into the follow-through.

Early in my career I came to realize how important it was to be able to do that under extreme pressure in major championship conditions. So what mind-picture best promotes this technique?

I like the one I settled on for its simplicity as much as its effectiveness:

Keep the palm of the right hand behind and under the palm of the left hand all the way through the ball and right on to the end of the follow-through.

Try This Figure-Eight Technique

A ROUND OF GOLF often calls for many less-than-full pitch shots, particularly in the 40- to 60-yard range. There are many ways to play these delicate shots.

Hitting downwind, or to a firm green, one option is to float the ball to the pin with a long, easy backswing and a relatively slow, soft downswing. The challenge here is maintaining the correct tempo throughout the action.

Another option, when playing into the wind or when you want the ball to run a little upon landing, is to grip down on the club, make a short backswing, and punch the ball. It's a good choice for a player with strong nerves and the confidence born from practicing the shot.

Another way to handle short pitches for golfers not happy with the above techniques is what I call the Phil Rodgers Figure-eight Method. It's named after my friend and longtime fellow competitor who taught it to me.

At address, position the ball opposite your left heel and set your hands even with it so that the shaft runs straight up and down, rather than leaning towards or away from the target. From here, swing the clubhead back slightly to the outside of the target line, with a full, free cocking of the wrists beginning immediately during the takeaway. Most important, let the clubhead drop back to the inside as you release it completely enough that it passes your hands through impact without them moving forward of their address position.

This technique allows you to use the bounce built into the bottom of the club, rather than the leading edge, to obtain height. It will take practice to build confidence, but, once mastered, will save you many shots.

In Bunkers, Change Set-up, Use Normal Swing

HERE'S A PIECE OF ADVICE for poor bunker players. The next time you are in the sand, use your normal swing with the set-up described below.

I suggest this because of the effect fear of sand seems to have on so many amateurs. They get in a bunker and suddenly they make 14 swing changes to get their ball out. The result usually is a lunge, stab, or lurch, with the ball either left in the sand or bladed over the green.

Instead, when playing a bunker shot, pick a spot a couple of inches behind the ball and try to make contact there. Concentrate on that spot as hard as you normally would the ball.

Now that you know where to make contact, set up with the ball positioned opposite your left heel, open your stance, open the clubface, shuffle your feet into the sand until you feel securely planted, and grip down a little to adjust for the lowered level of your feet.

Go ahead and make your normal golf swing as smoothly as you know how. I think the results will please you.

Visualize Removing a Rectangle of Sand

RELATIVE TO OTHER ASPECTS of golf, bunkers gave me trouble from the day I took up the game. It was always a big effort to make myself hit the sand, not the ball, chiefly, I'm sure, because I never had a clear enough picture of exactly where to hit the sand.

Things got easier when, instead of hitting into the sand at a certain point, I began to focus on an entire area of sand.

What I did was visualize a rectangle about six inches long and three wide, with the ball sitting in its middle. Then I visualized removing the rectangle, the ball simply going along for the ride.

These mind-pictures handed out a bonus. I discovered I could make the ball go shorter or farther by varying the depth of slab I cut, or by removing the same size slab but swinging softer or harder.

Pitch from the Rough with Your Right Hand

ONE OF THE HARDEST SHOTS for me has always been the short pitch from rough around the green. The bunkerlike, figure-eight lobbing technique Phil Rodgers taught to me some years ago (see page 116) is fine from the fairway, but I'm inconsistent from heavy rough, which adds loft to the club at impact.

Working with Rick Smith, one of golf's best young teachers, I came across a method he'd developed with my son, Gary, that gives me better clubhead speed at impact while maintaining the loft that I want for each shot.

Rick's and Gary's technique is to swing the clubhead up and down on the same arc and plane, which is kept as straight back and straight through as possible—no maneuvering the club either outside or inside the target line. At the same time, the steepness necessary for clean impact is achieved by cocking the wrists straight off the ball, then aggressively swinging the clubhead down and through the ball predominantly with the right hand.

When practicing this technique, be sure to hit mostly with your right hand, so that at impact you match the loft you established at address by fully "restoring the radius" of the swing. If you get too much left hand into the shot you'll slow the clubhead; instead, just let your left hand go along for the ride.

Learn the Late Riser

SO THERE YOU ARE, about a 9-iron from the green, but with a low-hanging tree limb blocking your normal line of flight. What do you do?

A popular option is to take a longer club—say a 7-iron—choke down, and try to adjust your swing to hit the ball as far as you would with your typical 9-iron.

I think a better option is to make a few changes to your set-up that allow you to go with the 9-iron and your regular action.

First, close the clubface slightly at address and position the ball farther back in your stance, with your hands well ahead. Then, set most of your weight on your left side.

Swing with confidence from that set-up, keeping your weight left throughout the swing. The ball should fly under the limb and far enough to reach the green.

Try the Woodcutter Shot

MY OLD FRIEND Phil Rodgers, an ace short-game teacher, has helped me a lot with the little shots over the years. Back at the British Open at Muirfield in 1966, he taught me a way of escaping from what seemed like an impossible situation in sand, which has saved me a number of strokes since.

The technique is employed when the ball is near the rear bank or wall of a bunker that is too steep to permit a normal swing.

Assume your normal bunker shot set-up and stabilize yourself for a hard hit by wriggling your feet deep into the sand. Once you are secure, simply pick the club straight up by folding your arms exactly as you would to chop an axe into a log lying on the ground. Then hit down very hard with your right hand two inches behind the ball.

Your objective is to shock the ball out by burying the clubhead in the sand behind it, so forget about a follow-through.

Visualizing the action as strictly up and down, woodcutter-like, rather than back and forth, golfer-like, will help you execute it effectively.

Skip It Up There

OCCASIONALLY YOU WILL HAVE a problem that appears to have no solution: ball sitting on hardpan with a bunker looming between it and the green, and very little putting surface between the ball and the hole on which to stop the shot.

The tightness of the lie prohibits wedging the ball high enough or with sufficient spin to stop it quickly. The bunker lip makes rolling the ball through the sand with a choked long-iron or putter very chancy.

What to do? Although it certainly isn't risk-free, a skip shot probably offers the best option. The goal is to one-bounce the ball from a level spot toward the front of the bunker so that it pops over the lip and up onto the green. Use a medium-iron, hooding the face slightly to give the ball a little hook spin. Stroke firmly using your normal chipping action and look at the ball hard until it vanishes.

You might be surprised at how well this technique often works out.

Get Down Low

HITTING A BALL that lies well below your feet is never easy, but it need not be as difficult as your instincts make it.

The tendency in the situation you see here, with the ball in a depression, is to lower the clubhead down to the ball by bending the knees. The problem is that excessive knee bend severely restricts the swinging motion.

Over the years, I've found I can partially lower

myself by widening my stance, and then bending my back. This way I can keep my legs fairly straight, permitting a little more freedom of movement.

The swing will still be restricted in size and force, so I normally use one more club—say a 6-iron instead of a 7-iron. Try not to be overly aggressive when you encounter this situation; it will help you to avoid wild shots and big numbers.

Use Same Technique for All Loose Materials

HITTING FROM PINE NEEDLES isn't the easiest shot in the game, but it's not as difficult as many amateurs make it. If you can escape from fairway bunkers effectively, you can do the same from pine needles, or any other loose material, using essentially the same technique.

Your top priority should be to resist any impulse to pick the ball cleanly, which generally results in thin contact and a line-drive trajectory. Instead, plan to play the shot just as you would from a good lie in the fairway, with three exceptions:

First, to prevent slipping, be sure to take a very secure footing, widening your stance if necessary.

Second, stay "quiet" with your lower body during the swing to further promote stability. To help you do this, plant your heels and keep them planted, much like you would for a fairway-bunker shot.

Third, to avoid moving the ball from its unsettled lie and incurring a penalty, hover the clubhead at address instead of grounding it (as I do on every shot to promote a smooth and deliberate takeaway). Then just go ahead and make your normal swing.

Accept Your Punishment to Avoid Disaster

EVER NOTICE what the top pros do when they land in horrendously deep or lush rough—the kind you see at U.S. Opens? Usually, they take a pitching club and hack the ball back to the short grass via the shortest or safest route. Higher handicap golfers, on the other hand, frequently try for much more than that, which is one reason their handicaps remain elevated.

On any shot from rough so thick that your first thought is "it's unplayable," accept your punishment and take the shortest possible route back to the fairway. Use a club with sufficient loft and sole-weight to fight through the grass, such as a 9-iron or wedge. Open the clubface slightly at address to offset its tendency to snap closed as the deep grass wraps around the hosel at impact. Hold on extra firmly with your left hand from start to finish to maintain control of the clubface.

Keeping your eyes on as much of the ball as you can see, swing back steeply, then hit down as hard as you can with your right hand, moving the leading edge of the clubface through the grass behind and under the ball. Forget about following through.

PUTTING

THERE IS PERHAPS no facet of the game that is more unique or individual to a golfer than putting. Turn on the television any given weekend and you'll see a variety of putters and putting styles—from the "claw" to the "belly." But, if a player can get the ball in the hole consistently, it shouldn't matter how unconventional or unorthodox his or her style might be—or is said to be by the experts. Idiosyncrasies aside, if it works, keep doing it.

I like that piece of advice because it points to what I believe is the single essential for great putting—"feel." Mechanics certainly play a part in putting, but "feel"—first for distance, and then for swinging the putterhead through the ball at the necessary speed—is, in my view, vastly more important.

Consequently, just about everything I do with the putter, in practice and in play, is about establishing the degree of fluidity between my hands and the head of the club that enables me to best "feel" the ball to the hole with the putting stroke.

Slight variations in the set-up and stroking technique play necessary roles in the process, but only in an effort to improve my "feel" for the swinging motion of the putterhead, relative to the distance the ball must travel.

Weigh Your Choice of Putters

WHAT KIND OF PUTTER should you use? The short answer is whatever works best for you. However, you may need a longer answer to guide you to the short one.

I believe the weight of a putter is the most important factor in determining its performance. There's long been a theory favoring light putters for fast greens and heavy ones for slow greens. Extend that to its logical conclusion and, if you play a variety of courses, you could end up with a dozen or so putters for the many speed variations you encounter. Even if this were practical, your confidence level would surely suffer from all the changes.

When I first turned pro, I used a light blade putter that I'd picked up in North Berwick while in Scotland for the 1959 Walker Cup Match. It served me well on the mostly speedy bentgrass greens used for the top amateur tournaments. It left my bag for good after five weeks on Tour. It was too light for the wide variations in putting surfaces I encountered in my first five pro outings, and I was in California the whole time.

The replacement was a blade putter built up to medium weight by a thick flange at the back of the head. That putter served me well for most of my career, but, even as I periodically made changes in later years, the new putters always have been of comparable medium weight, which has given them the same general "swinging feel."

If all of your golf is on fast or slow greens, you might well do best with a particularly light or heavy putter. But, if you get around a lot, I strongly recommend a happy compromise when it comes to weight.

Work Hardest on Speed

SINCE MY SONS are all good players with excellent vision, I confer with them on putts when they carry the bag for me. Otherwise, I prefer to read the greens myself.

Why do I like to decide on my own? Because the line of every putt depends on the speed at which the ball is rolled, and since the player alone controls speed through the force of the stroke, only he or she can determine how much break to play.

It takes some practice to figure out how effort relates to distance, but this should be your primary objective on middle-to-long-range putts. Look at where you usually miss these putts; chances are, you misjudge the distance more than the direction. In fact, most amateurs would do well to work on speed control over anything else when their putting goes sour.

It's also important to have a realistic approach to putting. We all love making long putts, but my objective from about 12 feet and out—particularly under pressure—is to leave myself a tap-in when the ball doesn't drop, which is most of the time. To help me gauge speed, I focus on rolling the ball at a speed that will put it within a three-foot circle around the hole. Haven't missed many of those 18-inchers over the years!

See Distances in Increments

BECAUSE THE SPEED of the ball's roll always determines how much it will break, judging distance—that is, the force of stroke required—is always the top priority in reading greens, especially with longer putts.

Some golfers try to compute speed on a long putt simply by obtaining a general impression of the terrain between ball and cup. Others will survey the territory from all angles, or actually pace off the distance as they look along the line.

Depending on the difficulty of the putt, I'll do all or some of those things. Over the years, however, I've found that mentally visualizing the distance in 5- or 10-foot increments as I stand behind the ball generally gives me the best sense of how forcefully I need to stroke.

Contours, turf condition, and weather all must enter into the computation, as well as a factor often neglected by amateurs, that is, the direction of grain. There are two basic rules in this regard: Bentgrass grows toward the direction of drainage, and bermuda toward the setting sun. On both surfaces, the grain is with you when the grass looks slick and shiny and against you when it appears dull and dark.

10' 20' 30' 40' 50'

AGAINST   WITH

Aim for a Six-Foot Circle

EARLY IN MY CAREER, the really long putt gave me more trouble than it should have. Eventually, however, I found it easier to judge the weight of stroke necessary if I walked all the way from the ball to the hole, and easier to see the line if I raised my eye-level by standing more upright at address.

What helped me most—figuring I wasn't going to make too many of these monsters anyway—was expanding my target from the 4¼ inches of the cup to a six-foot-deep circle around it. When I started actually "seeing" the circle in my mind's eye, then stroking to let the ball die just over its front edge, the improved results I achieved made me a lot less anxious about these putts.

That more realistic target "picture" might do the same for you.

Try "Spot" Putting on Shorties

OVER THE YEARS, I've rarely "spot putted," a technique where you pick a specific spot on the green as an aiming point. I prefer instead to visualize the overall line in my mind's eye. This method has proved best for me in judging the speed necessary to get the ball to the hole. On occasion, however, spot putting has helped me with short putts, as it might help you.

There are two spot-putting techniques that I've tried. The first involves picking a mark on the green a few inches ahead of the ball on the line you intend to start the putt on. The second method is to pick a spot a few inches short of the hole to roll the ball over. Try both techniques and consider using whichever one works best for you.

Committed spot putters claim that aiming at a spot much smaller than the 4¼-inch hole helps them roll the ball with greater accuracy. Other proponents say it helps them become less fixated on the hole, allowing them to make a freer, more relaxed stroke. Either way, it's worth a try.

"Unweight" Your Putter for Smooth Takeaway

THE SCIENTISTS TELL US a putted ball always skids a little bit before it starts rolling. Be that as it may, I putt best when I have the feeling I'm starting the ball rolling end over end the moment it leaves the putterface.

To obtain that feeling I have to swing the putter back close to the ground. In trying to do that, though, there's often a fear of stubbing the blade. The solution for me lies in a mental image and physical sense of "unweighting" the putter just before I start it back by raising its head just barely off the ground.

In addition to promoting a low-to-the-ground stroke, this little move helps me keep my body still and makes it easier to start the club back smoothly.

Match Heel and Toe for Squarest Stroking

GOOD PUTTING demands squareness of blade and stroke—that is, the putterhead swinging directly along the target line as it moves back and through the ball, with its face looking directly down that line.

I find I best achieve both requirements when I visualize making the heel of the club travel the same distance as the toe as I mentally rehearse the stroke, then actually see that happening in my peripheral vision as I make the stroke for real.

One of the most common causes of poor putting is closing the face of the club through the ball, which invariably pulls the head to the inside of the target line too quickly.

If you're guilty of it, I think you'll find my "heel picture" helpful.

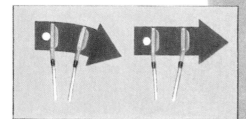

Improve Balance to Stop Body Movement

PETE EGOSCUE, the anatomical functionalist I've worked with for many years on conditioning myself for both golf and a better quality of life off the course, insists that the ability to achieve and sustain perfect balance is what separates the great athletes from the merely good ones. He's certainly convinced me of the importance of balance in all aspects of golf.

Last winter, I helped three amateur friends almost miraculously improve their putting. I did this simply by getting them to focus much more heavily on balance. The only thing I told them was this: "Set your weight on the balls of your feet."

The most common fault in putting, particularly among amateurs, is moving the body around during the stroke. Setting the weight on the balls of your feet makes it harder to move around, because you become more conscious of the need to stay still to retain your balance.

Give it a try if you're not rolling those putts as well as you'd like.

Try the same technique on your full shots, particularly if you are excessively active with your body.

Your weight will naturally move more toward your heels as you swing back and through, but setting up with it primarily on the balls of your feet will teach you a lot about address positioning and posture, as well as balance.

Pretend Your Puttershaft Is Glass

I PUTT MY BEST when I have a sense of gentleness in my hands, my stroke, and the way the ball comes off the putterface. Then the ball rolls consistently, which might just be the secret to fine putting.

To promote those feelings, I visualize the puttershaft as being extremely limber, almost as flexible as a length of rope, which means the only way I can get the clubhead to swing truly is to stroke very softly, smoothly, and slowly. If the limber shaft image doesn't seem to be working, I'll replace it in my mind's eye with a delicate glass shaft that will shatter if I'm even a tiny bit harsh at the ball.

Vital to swinging the putter this gently, but with sufficient speed to roll the ball the required distance, is a very light grip. Equally important is retaining that softness in the fingers throughout the stroke—in other words, no involuntary grabbing once you've set the club in motion.

Putt Like a Piston

TO ME, THE PUTTING STROKE is basically a right-handed action. I swing the putter back with my right hand, and I swing it through the ball with my right hand. All my left hand does is serve as a guide to steady and stabilize the stroke.

Visualizing my right forearm working like a piston is an image that helps me in using my right hand correctly throughout the stroke.

To "see," set up for, then sense the pistonlike motion, I need to bend far enough over the ball to position my right forearm horizontal to the ground, or fairly close to that alignment. The set-up also requires positioning the palm of my right hand so that it looks squarely at the starting line of the putt. The feeling I then seek during the stroke is simply one of my right forearm pulling back and pushing through like a piston.

If you're not putting as well as you like, try this piston "picture" and motion.

Stroke Slightly Upward on Bumpy Greens

EVEN WHEN STROKED PERFECTLY, a golf ball always skids a little bit before it begins rolling, the distance of the skid depending on the force of the hit determined by the length of the putt.

On bumpy or spiked-up greens, the tendency for the ball to be deflected by an irregularity is greater while it's skidding than after it has developed sufficient inertia to roll end over end. And, of course, the earlier the ball is knocked off-line, the bigger the directional error at the end of its journey.

Although a more lofted putter will sometimes help to minimize skidding, physics dictates that there is no total antidote to this problem. A partial solution used by many Tour pros, myself included, is to start the ball rolling as early as possible by positioning it a little more forward at address, then striking it just past the bottom of the putterhead's arc, or slightly on the upswing.

Give this technique a try the next time the greens are not up to par.

Quit the "Flick" to Beat the Yips

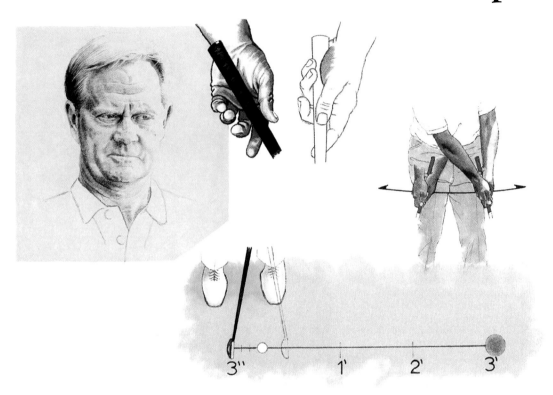

AN OLD FRIEND OF MINE, Memorial Tournament General Chairman Pandel Savic, was once afflicted with a case of the yips. Like many with that dreaded putting disease, he was making a short, quick backstroke, then flicking at the ball with his hands. This move was distorting both the putterhead's path and the alignment of the putterface at impact.

To overcome these faults and begin his recovery, I had him set the putter handle firmly against the thumb pad of his left hand, rather than in the fingers. I then told him to focus on swinging the grip end of the putter rather than the head—to the point of not even looking at the putterhead as he practiced stroking putts.

Finally, I suggested that he work at swinging the putterhead back one inch for every foot of green he needed to roll the ball, and to follow through the same distance. For example, on a three-foot putt the putterhead would move three inches away from the ball and then three inches past impact. This served to lengthen and further smooth his stroke, eliminating any remaining tendency to jerk the putter back or jab at the ball.

If you're suffering from the yips, try these simple exercises. They may help you regain your form on the greens.

Beware of Over-Practicing Putting

I'VE NEVER BELIEVED that quantity of practice alone will make a golfer a good putter. Without feel, touch and timing, I would not have holed the ball when it mattered, regardless of how many hundreds of putts I'd hit on a practice putting green.

Consequently, I've never practiced putting beyond a point where I knew I was doing what I wanted to with my stroke. This goal has always been the product of constant rhythm or tempo, marked by the putterface making solid and square contact with the ball. The physical feel and the mind-picture this produces is one of great fluidity between my hands and the putterhead.

Once I attain these goals in a practice session, I quit, even if I have stroked only a handful of putts. By continuing beyond that point, I risk becoming too mechanical or losing my sense of touch. You, too, should beware of spoiling a good thing by overdoing it.

Try My Putting "Musts"

A FRIEND RECENTLY ASKED ME to short-list my "musts" for good putting. Having tried so many variations on the greens during my career, it took a bit of thought, but here's what I finally came up with:

- Having the knowledge and patience to correctly read greens.
- Understanding that speed always determines line.
- Being comfortable at address (good balance).
- Setting the eyes directly over the starting line so the brain can "see" the putt accurately.
- Controlling the stroke with the wrists and arms (at least, that's what has worked for me).
- Making sure the leading hand guides the stroke, while the trailing hand delivers the hit.
- Holding the puttershaft vertically (from face-on view) at address and impact.
- Keeping the putterhead low to the ground back and through.
- Continuing the follow-through along the target line.
- Keeping the head and body still during the stroke. (Holding my breath as I stroke helps me to achieve both.)
- Most critical of all: having a positive attitude. Believe you can make 'em and you frequently will. Believe you can't, and you generally won't.

HOLE 18
YARDS 543
PAR 5

THE MIND GAME

WHEN MOST PEOPLE think of the mind in relation to golf, it's in terms of emotions or attitudes—confidence and patience being among the positives, and fear and anger as negatives. There is no question that such factors influence every player's level of success or failure at least as much as his or her physical performance.

Another and equally important element of the Mind Game, however, is what might be called "tricks of the trade"—practical tips on how to mentally handle specific technical aspects of the game and decision-making situations you will encounter throughout a round. To pick the simplest example, for instance, you should always strive to know the exact yardage on a shot, in order both to club yourself correctly and to determine the type of swing you will need or attempt to make.

To close this collection of MY GOLDEN LESSONS, we've chosen 15 such aspects of the game, where practical knowledge, born through decades of experience, will hopefully contribute to better play, lower scoring, and, in the end, greater enjoyment of this wonderful game.

Know Your Yardages

AS A YOUNGSTER, Deane Beman, now the former PGA Tour and Senior Tour commissioner, was one of the best amateur golfers in the world, not least because of his competitive smarts. I learned a lot from Deane over the years, but his best lesson came at the U.S. Amateur at Pebble Beach in 1961.

Although striking the ball beautifully, I was having trouble in practice judging distances of approach shots, particularly when the wind got up. Eventually, Deane said to me, "Why don't you do what I do—pace off the yardages and write them down?" I believe Gene Andrews, the fine California amateur, was the first to figure and record exact distances, but savvy little Deane was close behind him.

I paced off Pebble Beach and won that Amateur with some of the most accurate golf I've ever played. From that day on, I've rarely hit a shot in competition without knowing its exact distance. Once I began to have some success on the Tour, other pros began stepping off and charting yardages. Today, it is standard operating procedure in top golf worldwide.

Do you know exactly how far you need to hit your approach shots, even on your own course? If the answer is no, you might be surprised how much finding out improves both your club selection and your confidence over the ball.

Simply step off and note down yardages to the front and rear of each green from a permanent landmark like a tree or rock in the area where your drives usually finish. With that information, plus an estimate of how deeply the cup is cut into the green, it's easy to work out how far you need to hit the ball.

125 YDS

25 YDS

Make First-Tee Nerves Work for You

WHAT'S THE HARDEST SHOT IN GOLF? Driving to a ribbonlike fairway? A fairway-wood over water? A long-iron from a divot scrape? A downhill, left-to-right putt on a fast green?

How about the opening tee shot?

Everyone is nervous immediately before beginning any round of golf that means anything, including me. The trick is to make the feeling work for you, not against you.

The more nervous we are, the more we tend to hurry to "get it over with." Beat that urge by consciously reminding yourself to keep things s-l-o-w. The South African champion, Bobby Locke, used to do everything, from getting out of bed to eating breakfast to tying his shoelaces, in true slow motion before a big round. Taking some deep breaths, preferably from the diaphragm, will help you relax. So will staying easily in motion, which you can achieve through some lazy swings with the driver or whatever other club you've chosen for the shot (it should be the longest one in which you have the most confidence).

Once you get on the tee, blot out all peripherals, like what's at stake or who's watching you, and focus only on an image of the clubhead meeting the ball super-squarely and solidly. Then, take your time setting up, be smooth starting back, and go ahead and replicate that mental picture.

Prepare for Longer Courses

THERE ARE MENTAL as well as physical hurdles to overcome in playing courses longer than you are used to, and there are ways to practice to counter both.

Years ago, when preparing for a big layout, I would play Scioto, my home course in Columbus, Ohio, by hitting all the approach shots off an amateur friend's drive. This forced me to play a lot of longer iron shots than I normally would have, frequently from challenging angles. I recall once doing this with a friend who hit only three fairways. It wasn't much practice for me,

but I shot maybe the best 79 of my life!

If you can't find a cooperative friend, hit normal tee shots, but then drop a ball 50 yards back from where the good ones finished and play approaches from there.

Don't make the mistake of believing that more practice with long-irons on the driving range alone will ready you for a bigger course. The more you have accustomed yourself to hitting farther for real—into actual greens—the better you will meet the added physical and mental challenges.

Don't Swing "Easy"

GOLFERS WITH FAST, hard swings are constantly being told to "hit it nice and easy," or to "let the club-head do the work." These common admonitions have been doled out almost since the earliest days of the game. Are they sound?

It's true that brute force has never made a fine player. Think of all those muscular strongmen you know who have trouble hitting the ball out of their shadow. On the other hand, it's never made sense to me to think of swinging easily on full shots; at some point, the motion becomes lazy and therefore lacks control.

My approach has always been to hit the ball as hard as I can while still swinging rhythmically enough to keep the club under control. Only then can I consistently deliver the clubface correctly to the ball. The swing thought that has most helped me do this is "hit it nice and smooth."

Club Yourself
for Safety First

NO ONE ENJOYS nailing the driver more than I do, and I also like to hit into the green with the shortest possible club. But there are many occasions when it doesn't make sense to let it all hang out from the tee. Here's a classic example:

The fairway is very narrow to start with and the landing area for a well-hit driver is further tightened by four severe bunkers surrounding the landing area. Having only a short-iron to the green, or a chance to get home in two if the hole is a par 5, might tempt you to go with the big stick. Resist this urge by considering how much harder the hole will become should you end up in the sand.

In situations like this one, I've always played whatever club keeps me short of the trouble. This strategy has contributed heavily to my achievements in golf, and it will save you strokes, too.

Use a "Funnel" to Beat Severe Cross-Slopes

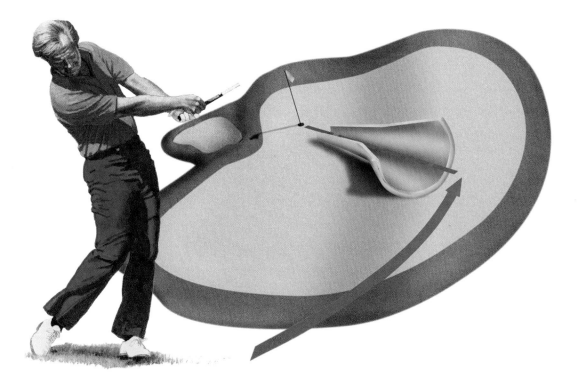

GETTING CLOSE on severely sloped greens frequently calls for hitting away from the flagstick and letting gravity feed the ball down to the hole.

A perfect example is the par-3 16th at Augusta National on Masters Sunday. With the super-fast green canted from right to left and the pin cut back-left, the only way to get within one-putt range—or even be sure of two-putting—is to hit well to the right and let the ball ride the slope. Because the target in such cases is general rather than precise, aiming and aligning correctly becomes more of a challenge.

My solution to that is to "see" the area where I want the ball to land as half of a funnel, then visualize how it will gather the ball and direct its roll.

Handle Doglegs with Your Head

SHARP DOGLEG HOLES often invite you to shorten the overall yardage by cutting the corners. Never hesitate to accept this invitation when you are swinging confidently, the carry is well within your capabilities, and the penalty for missing is not overly severe.

Even when caution prevails, you should at least try to pick up some extra yardage by shaping the tee shot to follow the fairway's curvature. When the hole bends from left to right, aim down the left side of the fairway and fade the ball back into the center. Conversely, aim down the right side of the fairway and draw the ball back to the center when the hole curves from right to left.

Can't intentionally fade and draw the ball? Well, you are an exceptional golfer if you don't naturally curve most of your full shots one way or the other—in which case you should cut corners when they favor your natural shot shape.

Experiment with Clubbing Up

IMPROVING EFFORTLESSLY at golf is a contradiction in terms—with one exception: club selection. Try the following experiment the next time you play a round of golf with little or nothing at stake.

On your tee shots on par 3s and your approach shots on par 4s and 5s, figure the club you need and then take one more. For instance, if the 7-iron seems the perfect stick, leave it in the bag and go with the 6-iron. When your mind says wedge, pull out the 9-iron, and so on.

As long as you make your normal full swing, you'll almost certainly score better. Here's why:

• You've gotten your ego out of the way, eliminating unrealistic estimates of how far you hit the ball.

• You don't have to make the "perfect" swing and hit the "career" shot that the shorter club often calls for.

• There is often more trouble in front of and to the sides of greens than there is behind them. The longer club will put you past the trouble, even with a mediocre shot.

If this procedure teaches you a lesson, namely that making realistic and strategic decisions leads to lower scores, then stick with it.

Beware of Over-Aggression

ONE OF THE MOST infuriating mistakes a golfer can make is suddenly shooting himself out of contention at the end of a tournament or match. The frustration is compounded when the collapse occurs because he took a chance by playing overly-aggressive shots that backfired.

For example, a golfer goes for the green in two at a risky par 5, only to rack up a big number by knocking the ball into deep trouble, such as thick woods or water. The reality is that even an expert golfer is unlikely to pull off a high-risk shot under pressure. Accordingly, the smart contender plays the lay-up shot that might set up a birdie, but that also ensures a par and keeps him in the hunt.

There obviously have been times when I needed to gamble to have a chance at victory, but being conservative when boldness wasn't imperative has earned me a lot more tournament victories than it has cost me.

Learn All You Can about Backspin

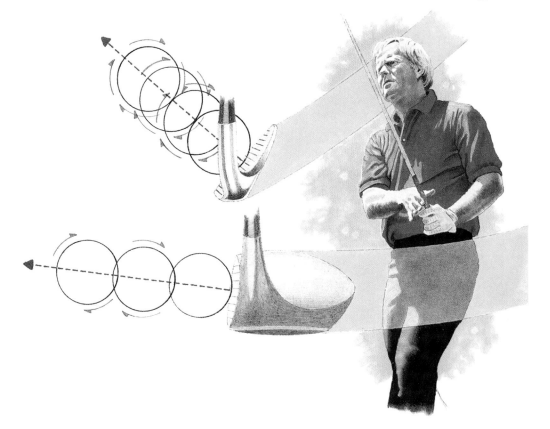

THE BETTER YOU UNDERSTAND the role of backspin in golf, the more you'll know about why your shots behave the way they do.

Backspin—when the ball rotates clockwise on the vertical axis from the player's perspective—is an essential element in ball flight. In large part, it determines trajectory: Every shot that becomes airborne has backspin. The more backspin, the more it rises, and the higher the shot.

The high-lofted clubs, such as the wedges, generate the most backspin. Their shorter shafts produce a steeper swing into the ball, along with a more glancing hit, and, therefore, greater backspin. The result is a high shot that stops quickly. The less-lofted clubs, such as the woods and long-irons, produce the least backspin, as the longer shafts produce a shallower approach, a squarer hit, and, therefore, a lower ball flight.

You sometimes hear of a golfer deliberately applying "topspin" or "overspin" on a shot. That's simply a misstatement. A ball with overspin quickly dives back to the ground, if it gets into the air at all.

Understanding backspin will help you predict what the ball will do in the air and on the ground. And controlling the ball is what golf is all about.

Pick Your Spot on the Tees

STRATEGIZING IN GOLF is about seizing every advantage within the rules and etiquette of the game. Paying attention to what might, at first, seem like inconsequential factors can add up to a healthy amount of stroke saving.

One example is where you position the ball for tee shots. Most higher-handicap golfers I play with simply walk out and tee up without apparent forethought, perhaps simply choosing the spot where the grass looks the greenest.

Instead, the first and most important thing you should do is find a truly flat area. Golf is difficult enough without giving yourself angled lies when you can avoid them. Fortunately, the teeing areas on most courses are uniformly even. If this is the case, you

have a choice as to the side where you'll tee the ball. When the most severe trouble is left, tee up on that side so you are hitting away from it, particularly if you tend to draw or hook your shots. With the worst trouble on the right, tee up on the right side of the tee so you are again hitting away from it, especially if your flight pattern is a fade or slice.

Factor in the wind. When it's across from left to right, tee up left so you can take as much advantage of it as possible, particularly if you can fade the shot a little. Do the opposite in a right-to-left crosswind, especially if you can hit a draw.

You might be surprised—and delighted—by the impact of such seemingly little details on your score.

Go for It When Conditions Are Favorable

IS THERE EVER A TIME when the less skilled golfer should throw caution to the wind and play aggressively? I believe so. This opportunity comes on long par 4s and par 5s that combine generous fairways flanked by minimally penalizing hazards—say, light rough and shallow bunkers as opposed to out-of-bounds or water hazards.

A perfect example at the pro level is the par-5 15th hole at Augusta National. There, the reward for a big drive is a chance to reach the green in two for an eagle or birdie, while a miss-hit rarely costs more than laying up short of the lake fronting the green and pitching on. Thus, nearly the entire Masters field goes for broke from the 15th tee every year.

Whatever your handicap, do likewise whenever the odds favor you. Going for your biggest drive or a long second shot when you are unlikely to be severely penalized is sound strategy.

It's also a lot more fun than always playing conservatively.

Make Your Mind Minimize Tension

HOW MANY TIMES have you lost a tournament, a match, or a personal best score, to tension? If your answer is, "Too darn often," here are a few thoughts for you.

It is not inscribed in any of the good books or stone tablets that you automatically must succumb to tension on a golf course. Correct thinking, plus a measure of self-control, will not only tame tension, but actually make it work for you.

You can overcome the "get-it-over-with, can't-stand-the-suspense" syndrome by consciously slowing down. Step back and take a deep breath, or two or three, while focusing your mind exclusively on the various practical factors—distance, lie, ground conditions, wind, hazards, etc.—that you must evaluate to decide your best course of action. Don't even take a club from your bag until you've done this clearly and conclusively.

Enjoy the challenge, which is presumably the chief reason you are playing golf in the first place. Thinking of past successes instead of failures will help you. If your situation suggests a shot that you've never hit successfully before, reject it and re-compute less ambitiously, choosing a play that you've already pulled off brilliantly. Replay that success in your mind as you step up to the ball.

Visualize. First see that brilliant previous achievement, then the shot now facing you behaving identically; picture yourself taking the club that will pull it off; then executing the necessary swing. As you finalize your setup, say to yourself, "Okay, I'm ready, now just do it," and go.

If you keep your mind this busy, you won't have time to get tense and pressured.

Listen Carefully to Sound Advice

ACCELERATE

ONE OF THE MOST FRUSTRATING and most enjoyable things about golf is that no one—at least, no one with any smarts—ever stops learning the game.

Struggling weekend golfers may like to think of top pros as impervious to the fluctuations in form that they suffer, but they're dead wrong. When a tournament golfer goes from four rounds in the 60s and victory one week to a couple in the mid-70s and a missed cut the next, exactly the same syndrome is at play that takes a weekender from a 95 one Saturday to a 110 the next. Which is, of course, that golf on any long-term basis is imperfectable by anyone.

I discovered early in my career that minimizing the scale of these inevitable form fluctuations

depended mostly on knowing my own game sufficiently well to self-diagnose and self-correct. But I also found that sometimes there was an easier and quicker way.

New tournament pros are often advised to stick with what got them on Tour and not listen to any of the advice that is so freely available to anyone with rabbit ears. Despite solid knowledge of my own technique, and a great teacher in Jack Grout, I did not adopt that attitude in my early Tour days. If I had a problem, and I ran across someone whose expertise I respected who thought he could offer a solution, I was always more than ready to listen. I might not act on the advice, but I definitely wanted to know what it was. And such counsel did, indeed, help me to many wins, including a number of my major championships.

The 1967 U.S. Open at Baltusrol is such an example. I'd managed to pull just about every aspect of my game out of some long doldrums except for my putting. Then, with only a day to go, Gordon Jones, a friend and fellow Tour player from Ohio, after watching me try all kinds of things on the practice green, finally stepped up and asked, "Jack, why don't you go back to the way you used to putt years ago? You know, take it back a little shorter, then hit it harder." I hit a few putts that way, then, suddenly, *bingo!*

The next day I went out and shot 62 in my final practice round, holing everything, and by the end of the week had won my second Open with only three three-putts to 17 one-putts.

Believe me, there's never any harm in listening carefully.

Find Balance Between Focused and Friendly

EVERY SERIOUS COMPETITOR has to find a balance between the innate and enjoyable sociability of the game and the need to concentrate fully on the task at hand—to be friendly and focused at the same time.

Here's the system that has worked for me throughout my career:

I will gladly converse with my fellow competitors during most of my walking time on the course. I like to switch off the talk and focus on my play as I get within 20 or so yards of my ball. From that point on, my concentration steadily intensifies. First I focus on the factors that will determine my strategy: distance, angles, hazards, lie, weather, and ground conditions. Next, I visualize the shot I believe most likely will be successful. Finally, I picture the swing necessary to create that shot, usually with the help of a swing key that will promote the desired execution.

Once I've evaluated the result and am on my way again, I'm happy to be sociable again—the more so, of course, the better the shot I've hit.

FOR BETTER PLAYERS

Some Extra Advice for Better Players

(and those who'd like to be)

HOW DOES THE GOLFER already breaking 80 most of the time get closer to par, or even below it? Here are some thoughts on that:

EQUIPMENT

It's fun to hit the ball hard and far, but keep in mind in selecting your equipment that power alone doesn't win golf tournaments.

Much hype has accompanied the hotter balls, longer and lighter shafts and exotic clubhead materials developed over recent years. Don't let it persuade you that you'll collect more trophies the farther your equipment allows you to hit every shot. Sure, more distance can help—so long as it's not at the expense of control. But there are other and often easier ways to score consistently lower.

Check out the country club scene and you'll find that the guys beating everyone's brains out are

mostly the players who happily drive 225 to 230 yards down the middle, knock it on the green more often than not with ample club and well-controlled swings, and, when they don't, own sharp enough short games to get up and down two out of three times.

Check their equipment and you'll find that it's fitted to playing within themselves and maximizing their confidence, not winning driving contests or slaughtering par 5s with wedge second shots.

CONDITIONING

However well you play now, becoming physically fitter improves your potential to play better. Greater strength and flexibility for better shot-making are the most obvious pluses. Increased stamina is another, particularly in terms of staying "up" for the full 18 holes or the entire tournament. Less obvious benefits are fewer injuries and faster recovery from them when you practice as intensively as necessary to play your best.

Having participated sufficiently at sports as a youngster to become a strong and healthy young adult, I gave little thought to conditioning until becoming fatigued by daily double Ryder Cup rounds when I was 29. From then on, watching my weight and increasing my work-out time unques-

tionably contributed to my competitive longevity.

Society in general is becoming more and more health- and fitness-conscious. Golfers not following the trend are obviously at a disadvantage to players who are.

PRACTICE VS. PLAY

The key to how much you practice, relative to playing the course, is to strike the balance that keeps you enjoying golf to the maximum.

Some people believe that intensive range work is essential to maximum performance, thus perform best when they hit enough balls to feel good about their level of preparedness. Others

compete best when they beat fewer range balls and spend more time working on the course itself. My advice is, figure out your most effective regimen, then stay with it.

The big danger for serious competitors is pushing themselves so hard with either practice or play that they become bored or over-fatigued—mentally as much as physically.

I avoided this in my best years by controlling my peaks and valleys. I'd compete, then, even if I was still playing well, discipline myself to rest and refresh my mind with other activities at home, then build up again with practice, then go back

out to the Tour for another week or two. Once I discovered how well this system worked for me, it became easier and easier to repeat it over and over.

As I've gotten older and my body has not allowed me to hit as many balls as I once could, I've spent more time on the course than the range. But, as long as I continue playing, I'll go on preparing myself to the best of my ability one way or another.

So should you.

INSTRUCTION

Instruction is a double-edged sword for many good players. I have a friend who, although well into his

seventies, has the health, the strength, the time and the desire to get from a 5 or 6 handicap to a 1 or 2, and who loves taking lessons in pursuit of that goal. But there are two problems.

The first is, he takes so many of those lessons, and gets so much differing advice, that he never sticks long enough to anything for it to work effectively. The second problem is that his body, at his present stage of life, won't physically allow him to genuinely change what he's ingrained for so long. The result is that, although still periodically playing around par, he's not consistent enough to attain his handicap goal.

The first message here is that there are no quick or easy fixes. The second message is that you have to identify your strengths and weaknesses and play within them to get the best out of yourself.

Can instruction help you do that?

Given a teacher who understands and accepts your personal parameters, yes, no doubt about it. Given a teacher intent on imposing some form of non-compatible "method" on you, highly unlikely.

The reason the "remake" or new method approach so seldom works, of course, is that, under pressure, we all revert to whatever in the swing is most ingrained or comfortable for us.

That's why I was so fortunate to learn a fundamentally sound way of playing the game from Jack Grout when starting out more than 50 years ago.

Compared to adversaries who began with faults that they were constantly pressed to fix, I never needed more than fine tuning or slight refinement to play my best.

TEE SHOTS

Just because it says par 4 or 5 on the card doesn't mean you have to hit the tee shot with the driver.

So control your ego.

As you assess what lays before you, decide on the club that you are most confident you can put

somewhere in the fairway if you are a good player, or in whichever area of the fairway sets up the best second shot if you are a very good player.

Actually talk to yourself internally as you do this, going through the bag in descending order:

"Driver?... No, not the way I'm swinging at the moment. Three-wood?... Still a bit risky. Two-iron?... Yes, I can get 2-iron on the short grass, and probably into that flattest area on the right, setting up the best approach, so 2-iron's the club."

Do that on every tee for a few rounds, regardless of how far your pals drive past you occasionally, then compare your "head-work" scores to your average.

You might be pleasantly surprised.

APPROACH SHOTS

Dead straight shots are the toughest to reproduce consistently.

Consequently, playing your best requires ingraining a flight pattern you can rely on for most of your longer shots: either a right-to-left draw or a left-to-right fade. (I preferred the higher-flying, softer-landing fade for most of my career.)

Simply knowing when to stay with your preferred "shape" going into greens could drop your

handicap a stroke or two. Here's how.

Including the par 3s, every good golf course features a number of high-risk approach shots in terms of green-side hazards, slopes, ground conditions, etc.

Coming to such a hole in a tournament and finding the pin positioned well to the right, I would try to cut the ball in close only if I was fading most of my shots consistently well that day. When that wasn't the case, I would play for the heart of the green and be happy with a par if my long putt failed to drop. The same was true if the pin was set left. Then, I'd opt for safety and the green's center with a fade, rather than try a drawn

shot when the left-to-right pattern was clearly working best for me.

Some people might call such strategy excessively "conservative." I call it playing within one's present abilities.

In other words, "smart golf."

RECOVERY PLAY

In pro-ams, I've seen pretty good amateurs try recovery shots that top tour pros would be lucky to get up and down once in 10 tries. Frequently, that compounds the original minor error into a disaster that knocks the steam out of them for the rest of the round.

When it's clear to me that only a miracle shot would get a chip, pitch or bunker play close to the hole, I accept the ball finishing 15 or 20 feet away, so I will be sure to two-putt if I don't "luck in" the first attempt, then go on my way with my composure still intact.

Remember, the laws of physics, quite apart from human frailty, make some shots impossible.

PUTTING

Insufficient attention to the speed factor hurts many good players whose putting doesn't equal their long shot-making ability.

To me, putting is almost all about the speed

at which the ball is rolled.

Get the speed right, first in your mental imagery and then in your stroking, and you'll instinctively "see" and start the ball on the correct line most of the time. Get it wrong and you'll rarely do either.

Realism is also important on the greens. Sure, we'd all like to make every putt we stroke, but it's never going to happen. For good players, accepting that fact might be all it takes to minimize, if not eliminate, the dreaded three-putts.

I'm never upset when I fail to make a putt of more than 20 feet.

Accepting how small are the odds of doing so,

my goal from that distance and beyond is leave the ball close enough to the hole to be certain of making the next putt—within eighteen inches to two feet. So my target then isn't really the 4¼-inch hole, but a three-foot circle around it. If the ball happens to drop, great. If it doesn't but stops within the circle, I've given myself a tap-in.

PUTTING PRACTICE

Work on "touch"—pace of stroke and pace of roll—much more than you work on mechanics. And don't over-practice.

Once you feel you are consistently rolling the ball the way you want to, quit and save your "feel." Ten to fifteen minutes is usually long enough for me to develop the sense of the stroke I want in my hands and the quality of roll that tells me I'm going to make my share. Keeping going beyond that becomes boring, which hurts my concentration. "Practicing himself bad" is a definite danger for the good player who feels compelled to work by the clock rather than results.

Finally, to complete your pre-round warm-ups, try my confidence-builder. Finish up on the practice green by holing three consecutive straight-in three-footers.

About the Authors

JACK NICKLAUS, with two U.S. Amateur titles, a record 18 professional major championship wins, and more than 100 victories around the world, is widely regarded as the greatest golfer of all time. In addition to his superb playing record, he has designed more than 200 golf courses, almost one-third of which have hosted championships or important tournaments in the U.S. and many other countries. A devoted family man, he and his wife, Barbara, have five children and many grandchildren. They reside primarily in North Palm Beach, Florida.

KEN BOWDEN has coauthored 11 books with Jack Nicklaus since 1972, prior to which he was the founding editor of *Golf World*, Britain's premier golf magazine, and editorial director of America's *Golf Digest*, the world's top-selling golf periodical. In the course of his extensive television and video work, he coproduced Nicklaus's highly acclaimed *Golf My Way* series. A low-handicap amateur golfer, he resides in Westport, Connecticut, and Jupiter, Florida.

JIM MCQUEEN has served as illustrator for more than 50 books, mostly golf instruction, as well as for the syndicated newspaper columns by Nicklaus, Billy Casper, Dave Hill, and tennis legend Stan Smith. He was also the Head Golf Professional at Mayacoo Lakes Country Club in Palm Beach County, Florida, the second course designed by Jack Nicklaus. He resides in Hattiesburg, Mississippi.

Photo Credits